CHANGE

the publishing CIRCLE™

Send permission requests to the publisher at:
admin@thepublishingcircle.com.
Attention: Permissions Coordinator
Regarding Michael J. Lopez

Published by The Publishing Circle
www.thepublishingcircle.com

CHANGE: THE SCIENCE AND ART OF TRANSFORMATION
FIRST EDITION
ISBN 978-1-955018-72-2 (PAPERBACK)
ISBN 978-1-955018-73-9 (LARGE-PRINT PAPERBACK)
ISBN 978-1-955018-74-6 (HARDCOVER)
ISBN 978-1-955018-75-3 (E-BOOK)

Book design by Michele Uplinger

CHANGE

Six science-backed strategies
to transform your brain,
body, and behavior

Praise

"I've seen firsthand how powerful the right strategies can be when it comes to changing your life, and Michael delivers exactly that. He's taken the science of change and broken it down into bite-sized pieces that anyone can use to start making progress today. It's insightful, actionable, and an absolute must-read for anyone ready to make a shift."

David Meltzer
Co-Founder of Sports 1 Marketing
Consultant & Business Coach, Keynote Speaker, Three-time Best-Selling Author

"A masterpiece in the realm of upgrading human performance. Michael beautifully articulates the difference and connection between the brain and our consciousness showcasing how this coincides with how we interact with the world. Powerful and transformative!"

Craig Siegel
WSJ Bestselling Author, Coach, TEDx Speaker,
Seven-time Marathoner, and Investor

"Michael has unlocked the science behind personal and organizational transformation. His practical, evidence-based strategies empower readers to make real, lasting change. A must-read for anyone serious about growth."

Lauren Johnson
Performance Psychology Advisor, Coach, and Speaker

"Michael doesn't just talk about change—he shows you how to achieve it. His thoughtful, research-backed approach will reshape how you approach challenges, both in life and in business."

Danny Creed
Certified Master Executive Coach, Three-time Author
and Seven-time Winner of the Brian Tracy Award for Sales excellence

"Change . . . has great information that is accessible to the reader. However, when you get to the strategies you begin to realize . . . wow. The strategies are comprehensive, easy to understand, and with desire, attainable to transform behaviors that no longer serve you. Combined with the change phases, you have a roadmap to healthier relationships, especially with the one that matters most . . . you!"

Dr. Nancy Dome
Author of *Let's Talk About Race and Other Hard Things*
and *The Compassionate Dialogue Journey*

Dedication

THIS BOOK IS DEDICATED to all the people that have helped, supported, and pushed me in my life. First, to my wife, Alex. Without your love, support, and encourage-ment, this book would not be possible. To Anyssa, Aidan, Ashlyn, and Lila: you inspire me to be the best father I can be. I've learned more from you than you realize. To Brian. For not only having my back for over thirty years, but for holding space during the most difficult times in my life. And now for being the best "guy-in-the-chair" anyone could ask for. To my coaches and teammates. I'm eternally grateful for the brotherhood we share and the lessons I've learned from you. To my parents and extended family. Thank you for always encouraging me to go far and strive. It's a message that has fueled me for as long as I can remember. Finally, to the colleagues, mentors, and clients I've been fortunate to work with along the way. Thank you for giving me the opportunity to work with you.

CONTENTS

Prologue

ONE QUESTION I OFTEN GET IS, "How did you end up doing what you do?" What I do helps individuals, teams, and organizations bring about change. Unbeknownst to me, I've been practicing change strategies my whole life.

And using change strategies comes naturally to me.

For as long as I can remember, I've pushed boundaries. According to my family, it first showed up as a cute, bordering on mildly irritating, habit of asking questions as a toddler. Most of the questions started with *why*. As I got into grade school, I remember asking my teachers the same type of questions. By high school, I had become an amateur non-conformist. I'd occasionally point out an inconsistency in a lesson. Or, my favorite, outright hypocrisy. But, for whatever reason, I seemed willing to raise my hand to challenge myself and those around me.

To this day, one thing I remember most about those early days was a comment from my high school chemistry teacher. Long known as one of the toughest teachers in school, people feared him. During one challenging class discussion, I kept raising my hand to answer questions when no one else would. Sometimes I knew the answer. Frequently I didn't. But I kept trying. After raising my hand again, he told me I wasn't allowed to raise my hand anymore. Someone else in the class had to respond. At first, I thought I might be in trouble. It turned out he was trying to teach the rest of the class a lesson. He said (I'm paraphrasing slightly since it's been over thirty years), "One reason Michael will be successful in life is not because he always knows the answer. It's because he's not afraid to be wrong." I didn't know it at the time, but it became a central element of who I am today.

By the end of my senior year of high school, my willingness to push boundaries—and not be right—started to pay off.

I played quarterback in high school. Heading into my senior year, my head coach told me I'd never play football beyond high school, let alone play quarterback. He said I was too small. I distinctly remember that being one of the most motivating moments of my life. Suddenly I went from being that little toddler who liked to ask "why?" to an eighteen-year-old who asked, "Why not?"

By the end of my senior year, I was accepted to Occidental College and offered a spot on the football team. At 5'7" and 155lbs, I did the thing someone told me I couldn't do. From that point on, I wasn't just hooked on pushing. It became my identity. And, as it turns out, just about every good thing I've learned as a leader and teammate resulted from my experience playing football at Occidental. My teammates were my brothers, and my coaches were like fathers. I can't imagine what my life would be like if I had listened to my high school coach.

The next push came shortly after leaving Occidental when I was hired as an Intelligence Officer with the Defense Intelligence Agency (DIA). About six months into my role, the United States initiated a military campaign in the former Yugoslavian states. Needing analysts to support the campaign, there was a call to support near round-the-clock operations in the Pentagon. You'll hear more about this experience later in the book. But suffice it to say, much like in chemistry class, I raised my hand for a job no one else wanted. And I became all the better for it.

After five years at DIA, I realized I wasn't really suited for government service. Let me say this: these were some of the most impactful years of my life. Much like playing college football, I learned so much about leadership, teamwork, and organizational performance from working with the military. But that same little kid who liked to push became frustrated by the government personnel system. So, I got my MBA and made the move to consulting. It was an important environmental shift that I believe fit both my working style and aspirations more closely.

This shift into consulting began my journey of helping clients think differently. Among my initial focus areas was risk management. Risk is an interesting topic because it relies on two important elements of the human brain. First, it requires us to envision alternate futures and (mostly negative) outcomes. Second, it requires us to make predictions about the likelihood of those outcomes. You'll learn more about predictions in this book. In addition, we often have to aggregate the estimates of many people together into a single assessment which is used to make important decisions.

It was here where I started to understand the power of individual core beliefs, as well as the limiting nature of assumptions and predictions. While these beliefs and assumptions were captured in terms of a project or business problem, they were rooted in everyone's fundamental beliefs about life. It was my first entry into the world of the human brain. More specifically, it was my first struggle with how and why the human brain affects and influences us as individuals, and then as groups. If that sentence sounds strange—"how the human brain affects us"—it's because it is. And that's exactly the point and something you'll read more about in this book.

I spent an incredible thirteen years with that first consulting firm. But, at the age of forty, I decided I needed a change. I needed a spark. While I had a variety of experiences in the firm, I suddenly felt a bit of stagnation (something else we'll talk about). I had come to learn my job so well that I didn't need to think about it anymore. I was on autopilot. I didn't feel (you guessed it) . . . challenged. So, my answer to that was to remove myself from that environment completely and place myself in a new one. One where I couldn't just show up and do the work. One that triggered a bit of uneasiness in me. I remember showing up at my new job and being intensely focused on this new endeavor. I couldn't just show up and do the work anymore; I had to really focus on it.

I also remember that being one of the first instances where I was consciously focused on leadership and culture. More specifically, non-aligned leadership and culture. Not that the company I worked with had a bad culture. It was just specific and, well, they weren't overly receptive to my "push" orientation. I heard the phrase "that's just the way we do things" quite a bit. First, I thought, why? Then second, why don't we change it? But the idea of change, of shifting, of doing something new . . . well, leadership didn't think it would work. So, we stuck to the script. I knew it wasn't the place for me.

After two short years, I left and arrived at Ernst & Young (EY). While this may be the inflection point of my realization that I needed to think differently, the arc of not just my career, but also my life, had been preparing me for the moment. From about 2016 onward, I helped many companies, large and small, try to transform. In some cases, we were changing culture. In others, we were changing technology. But, at the root of each of these cases was an established set of behaviors that people exhibited that made the work both fascinating and often frustrating.

Woven into this professional journey was my personal journey. Not long after joining EY, my family and I had to navigate the difficult transition of a divorce. Thankfully, we have all come a long way. It is important that I acknowledge the work my ex and I have done to continue raising our children. We are strong co-parents and for that I'm deeply grateful. While I didn't realize it at the time, most, if not all, of the strategies in this book have been essential to successfully managing this complex life. This includes getting re-married to an incredible woman and integrating new children into our blended family. As the first line of the dedication for this book notes, I cannot say enough about how grateful I am.

In addition, my time as an athlete, and now coach, became a central component of my identity. Coaching isn't just an opportunity to give back to a game that gave me so much. It is a chance to raise young men, build teams, compete, and, most importantly, pass along the life lessons that guided me. And, if you haven't guessed it, it is a place to push. To push myself to always be a better coach and to push others to be better versions of themselves.

It was around this time that the Venn diagram of my life started overlapping. Being a husband, father, co-parent, parent, coach, and consultant all came together. I realized the strategies I was putting into practice on the field were the same ones I was using in the boardroom. And yet, I was also aware of the fact that we would apply a deep understanding of the science of change and adaptability in athletes to help them learn and perform, then show up to work and go about helping people learn and perform in completely different ways. As much as the story you'll read in the Introduction was the light bulb moment that resulted in this book, my life as an athlete and coach has laid the foundation for my role as a change leader.

That brings us to what you are about to read. To say that this is my life's work would imply that I have nothing left to discover. As you'll see in the book, change is possible throughout our lives. I didn't start my first company until I was fifty. Wrote my first book at fifty-one. And, honestly, I feel like I'm just getting started.

My goal for this book is to re-frame your perspective about the strategies and techniques that create real, lasting change. This first requires understanding ourselves and others at a fundamentally new level. We must understand our biology, physiology, and brains in new ways.

In the Introduction, we'll discuss a brief history of change management, as well as a case study from the COVID pandemic that illustrates the true nature of change. In Chapter 1, we'll cover the foundational scientific principles that govern our experience of change. Chapters 2 through 7, we will dive into the six strategies that promote change within us. Finally, chapters 8 through 12 will give you a four-phased process to put your new comprehension into practice.

It is important to note that I do not believe you need to be a medically trained neuroscientist to understand these concepts. I've endeavored to take the research of the leading scientists and distill it into digestible practices that you can apply in your life. We have access to more research, science, and synthesized understanding of the human condition than at any other time in human history. We only need to apply the information that already exists. In addition, it is also important to note that nothing in this book equates to medical guidance or recommendations. As always, please consult with your medical provider before starting any new practices.

While writing this book, someone asked me an incredibly powerful question: "Who do you want to the reader to be when they finish reading the book?" I hadn't considered that question when I started. Upon reflection, my answer is simple. I want you to be someone that believes change isn't just possible. But also, that it's necessary. And then, I want you to start.

Change is, for each of us, a deeply personal experience, one informed by our unique history, physiology, family, culture, experience, and so on. By exploring the concepts and strategies described in this book, you will find a new formula for how to create change. And while I believe deeply that there is a formula for change, change is not formulaic. My hope is to give you the variables to build your own equation. And then, to give you the inspiration to create your own transformational work of art.

Introduction

I REMEMBER THE EXACT MOMENT I realized we needed to think differently about change.

It was the spring of 2017. I was sitting in a training for a soon-to-be launched software system at the company I worked for at the time, Ernst & Young (EY). Fifty people, managers and above, sitting through a four-hour training session. The training session was organized by a team of learning professionals designed to "get us ready" to adopt the system once it went live. The first hour was a presentation on why the system was important and how it contributed to our North American strategy. Increased data visibility, cost competitiveness, and rapid proposal response were all elements of the value proposition. The second hour, we opened our laptops and followed along to log into our accounts and navigate the basic functions. From there, we were each given a detailed spreadsheet outlining a variety of actions to take in the system. Add a new record. Open a new pricing model. And so on. We were to execute the action, record any issues, ask questions, and practice.

However, as 19th German Field Marshall Helmuth von Moltke famously said, "No plan ever survives contact with the enemy." During the opening presentation, numerous interruptions occurred. People stepped out to "take an urgent call." During the initial technical sessions, people experienced computer issues. During the spreadsheet testing period, many people were distracted by email. Some people simply never showed up for the training. Then, to top it all off, the launch of the system was delayed by another four months, which means that anything we might have learned in that half-day session was long forgotten amidst the countless meetings, emails, discussions, and travels.

First, let me say that the above training was done with the best of intentions. But, as I often say, there is no such thing as perfect actions, only perfect intentions. But the activities didn't actually help people change. When I looked around at the trainees, there were fifty unique individuals, all contending with different goals, jobs, and, most importantly, life experiences. Yet we were putting them all through the same experience.

This experience, which was preceded by several other similar experiences, unlocked a deep curiosity in me. To this point, most frameworks and methods for change were either the organizational change management techniques characterized by the story above or methods and concepts in the personal development or life-coaching space. These were my two choices for helping individuals, teams, and organizations change.

Organizational Change Management (OCM) is a relatively recent phenomenon. In the 1930s, Kurt Lewin published two articles that established an early three-phase structure for addressing change in groups. In the 1960s, change management models began to emerge from grief models, largely structured around the human concepts of loss that result from change. During this time, Everett Rogers published his work, *The Diffusion of Innovations*, a theory of how movements occur in groups that is still widely leveraged in the change community today. The professionalization of change management gained speed in the 1980s. Between what was then the "big six consulting firms" and the expansion of General Electric management principles pioneered by Jack Welch, formal processes to "manage change" in organizations began to take root. In the 1990s, a series of publications by Peter Senge, William Bridges, Daryl Conner, and John Kotter led to the creation of the ADKAR® model by Jeff Hiatt in 1995. ADKAR®—which stands for "Awareness-Desire-Knowledge-Ability-Reinforcement" remains the most well-known and widely used organizational change management framework to this day.

Unfortunately, the results of OCM have been less than stellar. As of 2021, the leading metric published by the consulting firm McKinsey indicated that 70% of all transformations fail. I've seen other metrics in the 90% range. A simple internet search reveals similar findings as far back as the 2010s. One study from 2016, "Digital organizational transformation issues, challenges, and impact: A systematic literature review of a decade," reviewed ten years of research to determine the critical elements to create change within an organization. Among the key findings of this study were that "to successfully implement an organizational change, a shift in actual thinking and behavioral pattern of the organizational members is required. This is because organizational change is primarily achieved through adaptive behavior of individuals."

If change is about people, we can trace the roots of personal change to 1936 and the work of Dale Carnegie, *How to Win Friends and Influence People*. Since its publication, the book has sold over fifty million copies and, for many, represents the dawn of the self-help and personal development industry. Back in 2017, when my own journey with change began, I will admit I struggled to sort through the wealth of content in this space. From success principles to visualization, to manifestation, to good old-fashioned leadership 101, the average person looking to change was faced with a daunting array of experts giving them "the secret."

As a practitioner of change, another ironic reality hit me. As a former college football player and lifelong athlete, I was ignoring the wealth of information and proven tactics to create metabolic change in our bodies. Despite decades-long research and results in creating physical transformation through exercise, diet, sleep, and the like, when we showed up to the office, all that learning seemed to be forgotten. The idea of "bringing your whole self to work" apparently didn't include an understanding of basic physiology and scientific principles.

This study in contrast prompted the realization that we needed to think differently about the problem of change. On the one hand, we were continuing to deliver well-established organizational change management frameworks that seemed, according to all statistics, to be underwhelming. On the other, we had an overwhelming wealth of individual approaches to change that were long on vision and aspiration, but hard to verify in terms of results. Neither of these considered much of what we know about modern day science and physical performance. This book is, quite simply, my answer to this problem.

A CHANGE CASE STUDY WE CAN ALL RELATE TO

The COVID pandemic created a tidal wave of unexpected change in our lives. Obviously, this type of change is a once-in-a-lifetime experience and, in many ways, is the exception to everyday change experiences. However, there were micro moments of change embedded within the pandemic experience that I believe serve as examples of, as I like to say, how change really happens. Let me state first that the COVID pandemic was clearly destructive on many levels. The use of this example is in no way intended to make light of the real human impact that resulted. Contained within the pandemic experience are countless stories of hardship and loss for which I am acutely aware and deeply saddened. Amidst this devastation are equal numbers of heroism that should also be acknowledged. This example is but one small illustration of change. Nonetheless, one that I recall contained deep insight for me as a change practitioner. The example I'm referring to is our adoption of virtual collaboration tools and remote work.

Prior to the COVID lockdowns, most working Americans worked in an office. Commute times and distance varied.

Then, in March 2020, all that changed in an instant. With millions of people now unable to go to the office, virtual collaboration tools have become the only means of connecting and working together. In-person meetings were quickly replaced with endless video conference calls. Many of them stacked back-to-back throughout the day. Our kids experienced the same shift, with school moving to remote instruction with virtual classrooms that provided lesson plans, tests, and so forth.

At first, the shift for workers was abrupt and, often, frustrating. Some people were on camera. Some not. Productivity, at least initially, declined as people worked to figure out both the new technology and the new collaboration rules of the road. For some companies, this lasted a month. For others, it was six months or more before teams settled into a routine. And in this arc were literally millions of individual change experiences, each varied and unique to the circumstances of the individual.

As this experience stretched into a year, something interesting happened. We adapted. People began to not only settle into the new routine, but they also became, in some cases, more productive (this is a hotly debated assertion). People began to navigate the new reality as they became more and more comfortable with the technology and the culture shift that occurred. Teams performed. People got promoted. Many people changed jobs! New roles and positions were created. Entire new companies emerged. And yes, in the time since then, many companies have experienced layoffs, some companies have disappeared. These are the normal perturbations in an economic movement that go beyond this brief example. But what remains is a new, hybrid working reality and millions of people that, I contend, would not have made the kind of technological and behavioral shifts without being literally forced to do so by the pandemic.

Multiple studies done since the end of the pandemic point to a rapid increase in our adoption of virtual collaboration tools. During the height of the pandemic, Zoom identified an almost 2000% increase in daily users. One study on the impact of COVID on the market for software-as-a-service (Saas) products concluded that the "pandemic has created an excess or abnormal consumer interest in the global web and videoconferencing SaaS market that would not have occurred in the absence of the pandemic." The studies on the true impact of the pandemic on working styles and preferences will continue to uncover new insights from this natural, global experiment. What is clear to this point is that the change experience has created a new normal that many people don't want to give up. What was once a frustrating change experience has become so common that millions of workers can't imagine going back to the way things were.

The COVID pandemic highlighted several factors that create real transformation. First, during COVID, our individual and collective environment changed dramatically. So much so that it removed the option of doing anything but using virtual collaboration tools. Second, during COVID, users didn't have time to "get ready" for the new systems. We all just jumped in out of necessity. Third, to the point of frustration, during COVID while we all experienced significant degrees of stress, personally and professionally, the magnitude of the pandemic created an "we're all in this together" mindset that channeled our stress into supporting positive outcomes. Fourth, COVID directed all of us into an intense focus on how to navigate the situation. This focus enabled us to work past the frustration so we could actually learn. Fifth, during COVID, we used the systems. Plain and simple. We worked through the setup frustration and personal discomfort. We often had help from colleagues in virtual shoulder-to-shoulder working sessions. And because everyone was in that same experience, we repeated that action several times a day. Finally, during the pandemic, the goal was to progress and maintain business continuity through new collaboration. A big performance metric or return-on-investment goal was never established. The goal was simple—to get people collaborating and working.

To summarize, virtual collaboration expanded exponentially during COVID because:

1. The environment changed. Substantially and rapidly.

2. We initiated movement into the new tools. We didn't wait. We moved.

3. We channeled stress toward positive outcomes. We embraced positive stress.

4. We committed to learning something new and focused sufficiently to learn it.

5. We generated repetitions over and over again. We failed and yet kept going.

6. We rewarded the progress of change instead of measuring the outcome of it.

This is how we change. If we are to be successful at changing, in any way, we must employ a combination of the following strategies:

1. Shift Environment—Shifting our environment can create positive, or negative, changes in our behavior.

2. Initiate Movement—We can influence our dopamine and how we define our change goals to create the motivation and movement we need to achieve them.

3. Embrace Stress—Stress is the adaptation of our bodies and

minds to change. Embracing stress can help us adapt and grow.

4. Create Focus—We need alertness, energy, and attention to change. Learning as adults requires specific strategies.

5. Generate Repetitions—Frequency, failure, and feedback are crucial. We must perform as many repetitions and errors as we can to facilitate learning.

6. Reward Progress—The brain's reward circuitry is built around striving. We must define progress differently, shifting from the nouns of our future to the verbs of our present, and make *effort* the reward.

These are the six science-backed strategies to transform your brain, body, and behavior.

Let's illustrate this by comparing the 2017 training story from the beginning of this chapter to the COVID pandemic. In 2017, the goal of the training I was in was to get employees, myself included, to use new financial management software for EY. This is called user adoption—defined as *the action or fact of choosing to take up, follow, or use something*. I liken this to learning to use your new smart phone. There's a process of figuring out the phone's basic systems and functions. It is the incremental process of *using* the phone. What happened during COVID was adaptation: *a change or the process of change by which an organism or species becomes better suited to its environment*. Adaptation is more than simply using something. It's shifting our behavior *because of using something*. For many of us, we start with adoption but don't always make it to adaptation.

When the pandemic first began, we collectively adopted new tools and remote working. Most of us remember how difficult that was. But what transpired, over time, was a lasting shift in our behavior that created a step-change in our individual and collective experience. We *adapted* to our new environment. The COVID pandemic accelerated adoption of virtual collaboration tools, which tipped toward an inflection point where behavior shifted. We didn't just use more video software. We adapted to an entirely new way of hybrid working that exists to this day.

While that inflection point for me was perhaps different from yours, when enough of us shifted, the inflection point happened at a macro level. Adaptation is change. Adoption is not.

Figure 1 represents this relationship between adoption and adaptation.

It's worth mentioning here the concept of stagnation. This is a term we are all familiar with thanks to economic theory. However, we, like the economy, can stagnate. Ironically, we often associate stagnation with a recessionary experience—a regression from the norm. The actual definition of stagnation is simply *a lack of activity, growth, or development.* We don't have to go backward to stagnate. We simply must not progress. Said differently, if we do not pursue adaptation, or change, we technically aren't standing still. We are, in fact, going backwards.

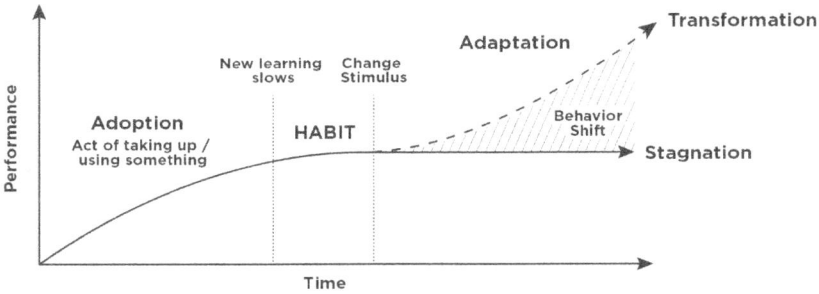

Figure 1: The Adaptation Inflection Point

Why do I share this distinction between adoption, adaptation, and stagnation? Because this is the challenge we all face, whether you are a leader of an organization or simply want to make a change in your life. To truly transform, we cannot go through the motions. Change requires us to adapt through a discernible and active shift in our behavior. It requires us to develop new patterns. Patterns which are, at first, incredibly difficult. But, as we'll learn and explore in this book, humans are perfectly designed to change. We are the most adaptable species on planet earth. We just tend to get in our own way when we do it.

Speaking of humans, let's talk about the foundational science that makes us the most adaptable species on earth.

CHANGE

Six science-backed strategies
to transform your brain,
body, and behavior

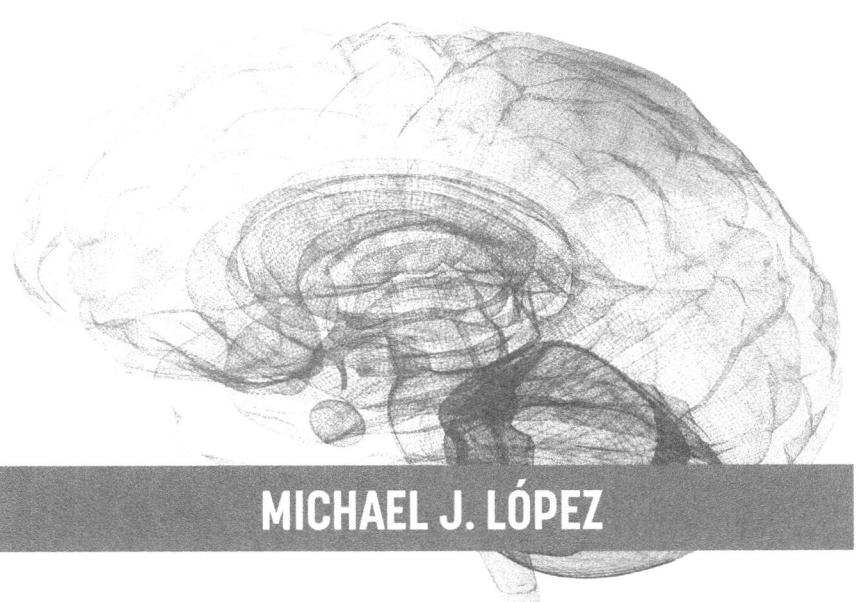

MICHAEL J. LÓPEZ

the publishing CIRCLE

CHAPTER 1

The Foundational Science

"Knowing yourself is the beginning of all wisdom."
ARISTOTLE

ENTURIES HAVE PASSED SINCE Aristotle first acknowledged that the search for truth begins with understanding ourselves. From philosophy to religion to science, we have continued this journey of understanding. While we are far from done, the reality is that we know more about the experience of change than at any point in human history. Beyond academics, a simple scroll through social media will uncover a multitude of reels, images, podcasts, and more, about change. From mindset to manifestation to cold plunges, we are inundated with strategies, tactics, and protocols to change just about any aspect of our lives. Yet we continue to struggle. This struggle stems from the overwhelming amount of data that can be difficult to sort through, validate, and apply in practical ways. It is, however, also due to the complexity of moving from understanding to the actual experience of change. Or, as I often say, "This all sounds great until you get actual humans involved."

In this chapter, we will explore four key dimensions surrounding the science of change. First, we'll explore that critical organ inside your skull. Second, we'll look at the relationship of your brain to the critical hormones that create the network of electrical signals and reactions we've come to learn as emotions. Third, we'll talk about the groundbreaking work in the field of emotions that is changing our fundamental understanding of how emotions originate. Finally, we'll return to the inner workings of the brain and explore the emerging literature around our thoughts and mindsets, with particular emphasis on the science of habits, willpower, and the neural pathways associated with learning.

In keeping with Aristotle's assertion, when we understand what's happening inside our bodies when we experience change, we are better able to move through that experience. This is not just an understanding of our thoughts, but also an understanding of the physiology of change, from hormones to our nervous system. If knowing yourself is the beginning of all wisdom, then it stands to reason that if we understand what's happening inside our bodies at a microscopic level, we can direct those systems towards positive change. And, as a social species, we can positively impact change in others, as well as absorb the scientific benefits that social interaction offers. In short, when we understand how people change, we change people.

THE BRAIN

If you haven't read the work of Dr. Lisa Feldman Barrett, you should. Dr. Barrett is leading the science of our understanding of the brain, and the vast majority of what you'll read below is based on her groundbreaking work. I hope to give you a basic understanding of the core concepts of what we have learned about our brains—the starting point for every experience we have. I encourage you to read her two books, *7.5 Myths About the Brain* and *How Emotions are Made,* for a deeper understanding of the concepts we'll explore below.

The first important component of brain science we should know is that, while there are regions of the brain that serve specific functions, each human brain is a unique network that is constantly building and re-building itself. For example, we know the frontal lobe is responsible for executive functioning and that it develops later in our teens and early 20s. But the pace, development, size, and connectivity of your frontal lobe is unique to only you. We can draw conclusions about general functionality, but the brain is a network without absolute boundaries. Because it is a network that builds and re-builds, it is adaptable. This adaptability is defined as neuroplasticity—the second important component.

Neuroplasticity is the basis for how we learn and change. Neuroplasticity occurs in one of three ways: neurogenesis, long-term potentiation, and long-term depression. Neurogenesis involves the creation of new neurons and neural pathways. This happens when we are young, and our fresh little brains are absorbing the new world around us. Neurogenesis is possible when we are older; it just happens at a far less frequent rate than when we are young. Long-term potentiation is the strengthening of existing neural pathways. Think of this as the doing-more-of-something-to-get-better-at-it process that forms those neural pathways. Long-term depression is simply the opposite of long-term potentiation— the weakening of neural pathways from under use or inactivity. Said differently, these two concepts of potentiation and depression are the brain's equivalent of "use it or lose it."

This network effect and the nature of how we learn results in an important characteristic of the human brain: it is a prediction machine. Your brain is constantly guessing, based on what you've experienced and what you've learned from that experience. It surmises what is going to happen next. The neurogenesis we experience in the early stages of life sets the foundation of our neural map. As we age, neural pathways strengthen and weaken because of our experiences and actions. The more we perform an action, the stronger the pathway. The brain learns that set of experiences results in certain outcomes and then anticipates those outcomes. The smell of mom's cookies, that tricky traffic spot on the highway, that "we need to talk" text . . . each trigger an expectation of what's bound to happen next. Faced with any scenario, your brain performs countless predictions, starting with the most likely, and it ultimately picks the "winning" prediction that then shapes your sensory experience and actions. As Dr. Barrett points out, ". . . an interesting caveat emerges here: your brain doesn't always aim for accuracy. [And] . . . There's also an intriguing revelation: your brain often acts before you consciously decide." It should be evident that this has dramatic ramifications for how we interact with the world around us.

Why is it important that we understand this about the brain? First, when making a change we must understand that no two brains, and therefore no two people, are the same. This seems like a "no duh" revelation. However, we have a tendency, particularly in the areas of organizational change, to presume that a strategy that works for one will work for all. Second, if we understand the foundations of how the brain learns, particularly as we age, we are better able to design learning strategies. It would be great if we could just soak things up like we did when we were young. Unfortunately, adult learning happens differently. Finally, and perhaps most importantly, when we understand that our brain is a prediction machine, we can better understand our actions and reactions, as well as those of others. I apply this insight any time I hear someone say, "That will never work." I realize that based on their unique brain network, specific neural pathways, and personal experience, their brain is in fact predicting that my new idea will never work. Why would it predict any differently?

THE BODY AND OUR HORMONES

According to Dr. Barrett, the primary responsibility of our brain is to keep us alive, and it does so by managing our body budget. Our body budget is nothing more than the management of resources necessary to ensure our heart keeps beating. This, depending on the circumstances of course, can be minimal or extensive. For our purposes, this is important for the following reason—if our brain is constantly predicting outcomes and making decisions before we are conscious of them AND it does so with the primary goal of keeping us alive, it will assign resources (in the form of hormones) accordingly. In some cases, that assignment is conducive to the situation. In other cases, it may not be. After all, your brain can only predict outcomes based on what it knows. As those hormones are dialed up or down based on those predictions, we can make the argument, as Dr. Barrett does, that our brains are quite literally manufacturing our reality.

With that, let's talk about four major hormones: dopamine, cortisol, serotonin, and oxytocin. Each of these hormones gets a lot of attention, and rightly so. They also get stereotyped into categories that, while helpful, have led to some misunderstanding.

Dopamine

Dopamine has often been labeled as the "reward" hormone. This is not quite right. Dopamine is the hormone associated with anticipation and motivation. It's more aptly labeled the "anticipation" or "pursuit" hormone. Many studies show that dopamine is highest not *after* we experience something, but *before*. The science of addiction is an extreme example of this. Gambling represents an example where the possibility of "hitting it big on the next spin" is what keeps people at the table. It's the anticipation of a win. As dopamine is heavily involved in anticipation and pursuit, it is a critical component of motivation. When our dopamine levels are high, we are more motivated to move and act in a manner consistent with acquiring whatever item or experience we desire.

Cortisol

Cortisol is often referred to as the "stress" hormone. If dopamine is the hormone that motivates us to move, cortisol helps recruit the resources, mostly in the form of glucose, to regulate our metabolism and create movement. This is particularly true in times of stress. As we'll explore a bit later, our relationship with stress has influenced our perception of the value of cortisol. More specifically, too much stress leads to too much cortisol, which is bad. In fact, it is our relationship to stress that influences our body's regulation of cortisol. Too much cortisol at night, for example, can severely impact sleep quality, which leads to negative health effects. However, higher cortisol in the morning is associated with increased alertness and focus. Cortisol and stress regulation have, for example, fueled the cold plunge craze. This leans on the idea that we can reshape our relationship to stress toward more positive outcomes.

Serotonin

Serotonin is referred to as the "mood" hormone. We often generalize that serotonin is involved in regulating our emotions. Serotonin, however, is involved in numerous physiological processes, including sleep, thermoregulation, learning and memory, pain, (social) behavior, sexual activity, feeding, motor activity, neural development, and biological rhythms. Thinking of dopamine as the hormone that gets us moving, serotonin is the hormone that helps us recover, largely through rest and sleep. Most people are familiar with the range of selective serotonin reuptake inhibitors (SSRIs) involved in the treatment of depression. For our purposes of understanding the experience of change in humans, the role serotonin plays in how we experience our emotions is critical. As we will explore shortly, it's time to think differently about what we know and understand about emotions.

Oxytocin

Oxytocin is referred to as the "love" hormone. Most know oxytocin for its role in childbirth and pair bonding, the critical hormone that creates attachment and connection between mother and child. We have learned that oxytocin also plays a critical role in releasing serotonin in the body, particularly as it relates to social interactions. As we'll discuss later, groups play a critical role in supporting our ability to change. The release of oxytocin, along with serotonin, is one of the rewards we gain from positive experiences. And those rewards can come in many forms.

What's important to remember is that while we can make general statements about the role these hormones play, they do not work in isolation. As just mentioned, oxytocin plays a role in amplifying the release of serotonin. Cortisol reacts in response to stress indicators, but dopamine plays a role in our willingness to engage in stressful situations. Your brain is constantly releasing these hormones based on stimuli and experiences unique to you. As a result, one person's "stressful" situation might barely register for someone else. One person's positive social experience, which releases oxytocin and creates a comforting reward, might be the source of someone else's extreme cortisol response to stress. What we know is that the amplification of these hormones creates internal experiences in our bodies, which manifest in what we call emotions.

EMOTIONS

As we learned in the previous chapter from Dr. Barrett's research, our brains control the assignment of resources required to keep us alive. This includes the up and down regulation of hormones, heart rate, glucose, and so on. What is groundbreaking in Dr. Barrett's research is that our emotions are not the trigger for how the body responds, they are the result. As our brain reaches back into our own experience, it gauges what the body requires and sends preemptive instructions to the body to respond. Think about public speaking, the experience many people often describe as equal to or greater than death on the fear spectrum. As you prepare to walk in front of the group, your brain begins to predict the range of negative outcomes you presume will occur. Your heart begins to race. Glucose accelerates through the body. Cortisol increases. Sweat production increases as a result of the rise in body temperature from an increased heart rate and glucose consumption. All of this occurs without our "knowing." We interpret and label the collective experience of these responses as fear. Or perhaps anxiety. Maybe you choose another word. But what's important to understand here is the cause-and-effect relationship of our emotions. Our emotion occurred because our brain made predictions about the future based on its experience of the past.

What's more, the intensity of our emotional response is a result of the accuracy of our brain's original prediction. If my presentation went well, then my brain got me all worked up for nothing and it will update its experience archive to potentially respond less acutely the next time I speak to a group. If the presentation went poorly, I can expect a more dramatic response in the future.

Why is this important to our understanding of how people change? Because it means that different emotions can happen for the exact same experience. How my body predicts an outcome and then uses up resources in one experience may be different from yours.

Imagine the experience of an untrained person responding to a fire compared to a firefighter. Firefighters train daily to understand, anticipate, and respond to a variety of dangerous situations. As a result, their brain learns and develops an archive of experiences that shapes how their bodies respond in those situations. It's not that they don't feel the rush of physiological responses. It's that they have developed a brain archive that creates a different emotional response than if you and I were in the same situation. So, while the average white-collar team meeting or blue-collar shift work experience does not meet the stress level of a five-alarm fire, what's clear is that each person's emotional response to the same situation can, and does, vary widely.

Added to this variety of emotional responses is the language we use to describe them and the culture from which that language originates. It was previously thought that a set of universal emotions existed—sad, happy, angry, etc. Research into the brain development of young children across cultures suggests that these are culturally-learned experiences that shape our understanding, and description, of them. Many of the words we use today are cultural conventions that actually reinforce our understanding and experience of our emotions.

For example, according to Dr. Barrett, the ancient Greeks and Romans had no word to describe "smiling" and she has shared that the word "smile" was created in the eighteenth century. In today's research, we see countless words used to describe the experience of "sadness." With countless words to describe a variety of emotional experiences that we each uniquely have, it's no wonder why we struggle to create change experiences that work for everyone when everyone is having and describing a different experience!

HABITS AND MINDSET

What this chapter should have reinforced by now is that a large percentage of our physiological and emotional responses are not within our conscious control. Our brain is working 24/7 to manage our body budget and regulate the physical resources that create what we experience as emotions (and in many cases define our reality). First stimulus, then brain prediction, followed by body budget allocation, resulting in an emotional response based on the accuracy of the original prediction. What we haven't yet discussed are the conscious thoughts, and the effects of those conscious thoughts, along that chain. Before we do so, we need to explore something we're all familiar with: habits.

Habits are an often-discussed topic these days. From the 2018 work by James Clear, *Atomic Habits*, to another expansive work on the topic by Dr. Wendy Wood, *Good Habits, Bad Habits*, we understand and appreciate the power of habits more than ever. After all, as Dr. Wood points out in her book, approximately 43% of what we do every day is a habit. With so much of our lives dedicated to autonomous activity, it's clear that we must approach the impact of habits, positively and negatively, when we consider change.

Let's first discuss what a habit is. *Merriam-Webster* defines a habit in three ways. First, a settled tendency or usual manner of behavior. Second, an acquired mode of behavior that has become nearly or completely involuntary. And third, a behavior pattern acquired by frequent repetition or physiological exposure that shows itself in regularity or increased facility of performance. In all three examples, we see some important themes—a pattern of repeated behavior, a degree of automaticity or sub-consciousness, and, importantly, context. A habit isn't just something you do often, it is something that you do often in response to certain cues and/or context. Almost any action can become a habit because a habit is not defined by the type of activity, but by how it's performed.

Habits serve an important role in our lives. When something is a habit, our brain more efficiently regulates the assignment of resources required to operate it. If we didn't have habits, each of our days would be spent tirelessly thinking, or at worst debating, about every action we needed to perform. With our brain being the most resource intensive organ in our body, habits relieve our brain of managing resources in one place to direct them to higher-value functions.

Why do habits matter when it comes to change? It all comes down to those higher-value functions. The fact of the matter is that change requires effort—deliberate and persistent effort to shift our behavior. The best way to think about this is as a spectrum, with habits at one end and change, sometimes called tenacity or willpower, at the opposite end.

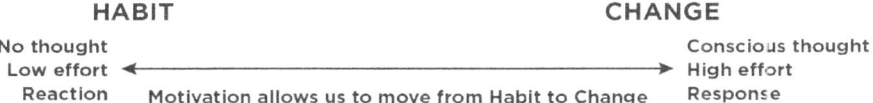

HABIT		CHANGE
No thought		Conscious thought
Low effort	←————————————————————→	High effort
Reaction	Motivation allows us to move from Habit to Change	Response

Our brain wants to manage your "body budget" to put as much in the habit category as possible. The challenge, of course, is that we often aspire to change, which requires that we break the structure of habits with intentional thought and effort. What allows us to move away from habits and toward change is motivation. Motivation, as we learned, is primarily (but not solely) the byproduct of increased dopamine. If you've ever made a New Year's resolution, you understand this experience. We make great proclamations to ourselves about getting into shape, reading more, drinking less, and so on. And yet, you likely also understand the experience of feeling motivated the first week of January only to see that motivation wane week by week. Enter mindset.

Over the last decade, the scientific community has engaged in a rich debate about the power of mindset. For many years, we collectively viewed motivation (or willpower) as a finite resource. In the late 1990s, Roy Baumeister, an American social psychologist, introduced the concept of ego depletion, the idea that self-control or willpower draws upon a limited pool of mental resources that can be used up. For years, we collectively believed willpower was a finite resource almost exclusively reliant on the level of blood glucose available in the system. Recall that our brain uses glucose for energy and if the brain manages our body budget, then it stands to reason that if I have more glucose in my system, then I have more available willpower, or motivation, to move away from habits toward change.

That view held firm until two critical studies reshaped our view of willpower as a finite resource. The first, a critical study by Carol Dwek, demonstrated that simply believing that willpower was not a limited resource significantly improved the expression of willpower. The second study, conducted by Alia Crum, demonstrated that adopting a "stress is enhancing" mindset is a distinct and meaningful variable in determining the stress response. Simply believing that stress is good for you increases your positive experience of the stress itself. We have come to define this as *growth mindset*. What the research into growth mindset has demonstrated is that, while we might not control most of our body budgeting systems or the emotional responses that result, we can direct our conscious thoughts towards improving how we experience change.

BACK TO THE BRAIN

Which brings us back to the brain and the final, critical element of brain science. It turns out that doing hard things, particularly things we don't want to do, is good for us. A 2020 study, entitled *The Tenacious Brain: How the Anterior Mid-Cingulate Contributes to Achieving Goals*, published by several neuroscientists, including Dr. Feldman Barrett, deeply changed our understanding of the benefits of tenacity. Popularized in the book *Grit*, by Angela Duckworth, this study was able to demonstrate that when we engage in activities that require us to persevere through challenge, a critical region of our brain, the Anterior Mid Cingulate Cortex (aMCC), increases in size. The aMCC is the superhighway interchange of the brain that controls critical activities, such as directing primary communication to other areas of the brain, directing spontaneous activity, executive function, and something called allostasis. Allostasis is a physiological mechanism of regulation in which the human body anticipates and adjusts its energy use according to environmental demands. This might sound familiar. Allostasis is the body budgeting process.

The study states that "the aMCC serves as a structural and functional hub of communication that synchronizes information from otherwise segregated systems . . . the aMCC's connections allow it to integrate information from multiple brain networks to drive goal-directed behaviors. In other words, its position allows it to participate in the willed control of our behavior." The aMCC is, in short, where the ability to change originates in the brain.

I hope you feel differently about the brain—your brain—at the end of this chapter than you did at the beginning. What might have felt like a process for which we have little control over is quite different from the reality. Of course, we cannot directly control our brain's autonomous predictions or assignment of resources, aka hormones, directly. We certainly can't control these processes in others. But we can influence the systems in our brain by (1) directing our thoughts toward a stress-is-enhancing mindset and (2) applying that mindset in directed, purposeful actions that improve the performance of our Anterior Mid Cingulate Cortex (aMCC), the functional hub of communication and resource assignment in the brain. We do this by engaging in activities that require us to be tenacious; activities that require us to persevere through hardship and do the literal "thing we do not want to do." In doing so, we train our aMCC to become more efficient, more effective, and more resilient in managing that autonomous prediction and body budgeting system. In short, the more we do hard things, the more we strengthen the neural pathways for doing hard things through long-term potentiation. The result is that we re-train our brain's prediction system to be less reactive to future instances of stress or uncertainty. Our future predictions become more certain and our body budgeting system more effective, stabilizing our emotional experiences and expanding our ability to change.

Let's talk about how we do that.

CHAPTER 2

Strategy One—
Shift Environment

"Motivation is overvalued. Environment matters more."
JAMES CLEAR

I
N AUGUST 1991, I LEFT for my first year at Occidental College in Los Angeles, California. Though classes wouldn't start until September, I was arriving early for the start of the fall football season. As is tradition for many recent high school graduates, we loaded up my mother's car with suitcases and boxes to make the six-hour drive from Sacramento to LA. The drive itself was unremarkable. It was the events that transpired when we arrived that would give me my first lesson (unbeknownst at the time) in the power of shifting your environment.

The arrival looked like most first-day college experiences. Arriving at campus and searching for the dorm. Finding the dorm and nervously asking if we were in the right place. Unloading boxes and deciding which bed to sleep in. Meeting my soon-to-be teammates during the check-in process. While memorable, the entire process was largely unremarkable.

Having wrapped up the check-in process, me, my mother, grandmother, grandfather, and high school girlfriend left campus to find some lunch.

We found a fast-food restaurant about a half mile from campus. My family had reserved hotel rooms close by, and the plan was to spend some time together that evening before they drove back to Sacramento in the morning. I had my first day of practice the next day. As lunch concluded, my grandfather walked first out the door toward the car parked just outside the main entrance. As he did, another car backed out of a parking spot and violently hit him.

I ran towards him as he lay on the ground. Thankfully, his injuries were not life threatening, but they were severe enough that he needed immediate medical attention. Within minutes, the ambulance arrived. They loaded up my grandfather. My grandmother joined him. My mom and girlfriend needed to follow them to the hospital. We all exchanged hugs quickly, and they hurriedly rushed off. And there I was. Alone. In the parking lot of a fast-food restaurant. I didn't know anyone and wasn't entirely sure even how to get back to campus. Cell phones didn't exist, so there was no way of even getting an update on my grandfather. Within what felt like seconds, my environment changed. Dramatically. Permanently. It was the first, and one of the most impactful, environmental shifts in my entire life.

I eventually made my way back to campus. Found my room. Told a few people what had happened. I quickly became the guy whose grandpa was "run over at the Wendy's." I unpacked the rest of the way and settled in for my first night. I was a bit traumatized from the day, yet excited for the next. What I remember most was the realization that this was my life now. There was no going back. No "other" choice. Let's talk about this concept—choice—for a moment.

It turns out that variety may not be the spice of life after all. Decades of research have consistently shown that the "paradox of choice" makes decision-making challenging for us. We tend to believe that more options are better, but it turns out that too many options make it difficult for us to pick the "ideal" answer. While this was originally research around product selection, we've seen the phenomenon occur from what to have for lunch, to what to watch on Netflix, to what potential date to pick on dating apps. In short, having more options leads to decreased satisfaction, lower confidence in our choices, and a higher chance that we will regret our decisions.

Now, you might think to yourself, *What does your grandfather getting run over in a parking lot and you being left at school have to do with the "paradox of choice?"* Well, it turns out that when we limit our choices, we not only experience more satisfaction in picking which option we choose, we increase our chances of how we then interact with that choice. For example, when my family left and I was alone in the fast-food parking lot, my decision space was not about what I had to do next—that was clear: I had to go back to campus and my dorm. It was about how I was going to interact with the new environment I was in. How I was going to interact with my teammates. How I was going to get ready for the first day of practice. And so on. When the environment presented me with constraints, my decisions were limited and, as a result, I moved quickly into action planning. This is where growth began. In the modern world of online dating, if there's always another profile to pick from, I don't really need to commit to a course of action with one. On that September day in 1991, I had *one* option, and it was to return to the Occidental College campus and figure out my new life.

We have tremendous opportunity to leverage environmental shifts in our lives, both at home and at work. We only need to embrace the idea that constraints are helpful levers to create change. The challenge is that constraints tend to not feel all that great. It requires designing our lives in ways that limit behavior options or, in some cases, simply remove alternative options altogether. While this sounds simple, our lives are complex and the inclusion of constraints in our lives affects those around us. At home, it can create friction in our relationships with both partners and children. At work in the age of employee empowerment, it can create culture impacts that could lead to retention issues. Nonetheless, the fact of the matter is that environmental constraints are incredibly effective behavioral modification levers. Let's explore a few.

THE PHYSICAL ENVIRONMENT

The clearest and most apparent environmental constraints are, of course, the physical spaces which we occupy. Since Charles Darwin first recognized the impact of the environment on the behavior and evolution of animals in the Galapagos, we have studied the impact of macro and micro environmental changes on behavior. Just about everyone on planet Earth experienced the most massive environmental shift we will probably ever experience during the COVID pandemic. The constraints imposed during the pandemic shifted economies, industries, companies, teams, and us as individuals. For many of us prior to the pandemic, our physical constraints began with a daily commute to a centralized working location, followed by a daily schedule of physical interactions, planned and unplanned, around which work was accomplished. Today, we've replaced that (although not entirely) with an ever-increasing set of video meetings, integrated work-life experiences with child and family care, and so on.

The design of our physical spaces has a large impact on us. Prior to the pandemic, the advent of the Dot-Com era created the campus-style office location, which created a network of services and amenities that made it easier to stay in the office without the interruptions of daily life. In the days since, office space has been reduced significantly, as has the layout of offices. Prior to the pandemic, executives had plush corner offices that clearly signaled their status. Now, many offices are occupied for only a few days a week and employees and executives simply find an open desk (called "hot desking"). While there are still some offices that operate under the old standard, hybrid working defines our experience. All these changes came about because of significant constraints that limited our physical movement. Those constraints lasted long enough that we permanently shifted our behavior to the point that many people don't want to return to the office. The debate around this has become fierce.

The good news is that it is not only environmental constraints that can prompt us to change. Creating environmental access also affects our ability to change. In this case, "access" is defined as the availability of resources or tools that prompt us to make a change. A simple example involves nutrition. If you want to lose weight by improving your diet, you might hire a nutritionist. One of the first things a nutritionist would do would be to go into your refrigerator and pantry and remove all the junk food. Then they would educate you on how to replace junk food with healthier options as well as how to position that food into easily accessible locations that increase your chances of grabbing a healthy snack instead of an unhealthy one.

Several studies have been done that demonstrate how the design of our physical environments can contribute to healthy behavior patterns. One such study found that well designed physical spaces can have both a positivoe effect on individual health and well-being but can also increase an individual's willingness to make choices that benefit that same environmental space. A 2022 study on post-pandemic workplace indicated that workplace design can have a significant, positive impact on employee performance. In short, our physical environments shape us.

THE VIRTUAL ENVIRONMENT

Like an animal that adapts to its new environment, these physical environmental shifts have migrated into changes in our virtual world. On the professional side, remote working and collaboration have spawned numerous technologies to increase connection and productivity now that we have moved away from as much in-person interaction. Tools such as Teams and Slack dominate the communication landscape, while technologies, such as Mural and Miro, are available for virtual workshops. And now, artificial intelligence (AI) provides even more capability for us.

It goes without saying that the virtual environment of social media has become the norm in our lives. It's not my scope here to debate the pros and cons of our increasingly virtual world. It is simply to acknowledge the grand scale of it. I could fill this book with statistics about the positive and negative affects of social media and virtual connections. For every statistic that might point to its deleterious effects, we can find stories of lives forever altered in positive ways through our virtual connections. What's clear is that we have both adopted and now adapted our behavior in these virtual spaces. That adaptation is not done.

Ironically, the same stagnation that can occur in our physical spaces and occur in our virtual spaces as well. Whether it is a custom spreadsheet that you'd rather use at work instead of that new fancy database or your penchant for scrolling your favorite social media app for hours, our inclination towards habit-based behaviors shows up here as well. It's one reason you'll hear of people taking a social media break by deleting the apps on their phone. This removes the option of accessing those platforms. Freeing up space for activities and behaviors.

Here's the harsh truth about our virtual spaces. Virtual spaces, such as social media, are programmed to keep us, well, *in* them. For example, much of social media triggers the dopamine system. We've already established that the brain likes dopamine. So, we keep coming back to that trigger. When combined with the simple design that makes opening and scrolling among the most involuntary habits you can engage in, it is the technological equivalent of a mouse hitting a lever for food. Many of these technologies are structured to quickly, almost imperceptibly, move you from adoption to habit.

THE EMOTIONAL ENVIRONMENT

Access is also a critical concept in our emotional environments. While we tend to think of our environment in two- or three-dimensional terms, the emotional environments we occupy have a tremendous impact on our behavior. We often understand the emotional environment as organizational culture—be that the tone set in a company by leaders, the emotional toll of a toxic coworker, or the freedom created by an inspiring mentor, our beliefs and experiences derived from our emotional environments are critical. Anyone that has worked in a "toxic" environment or, unfortunately, has grown up in an emotionally challenging home, understands just how damaging the sustained impact of chronic negative emotions can be. Research has been done on this topic for decades, the most famous of which was Google's landmark research, Project Aristotle. This research uncovered that the single most important element of team success was psychological safety, followed by dependability, structure, and clarity, meaning, and impact. This environment of psychological safety was not dependent on location or physical variables. It was, quite simply, a collective sense of safety. Safety to ask questions. Safety to experiment. Safety to fail. Sadly, we've all experienced the opposite of these concepts at some point in our careers. In more damaging cases, negative emotional environments show up as real trauma, which can sadly have long-lasting effects.

Here's a short example. During the pandemic, I was leading the implementation of a customer relationship management (CRM) system for my firm. Implementing a CRM system is difficult. This project was no different. Under the best of circumstances, implementing a new piece of software for over 14,000 people is daunting. From redesigning business processes to training new skills to shifting behaviors for leaders and teams, a CRM system will create stressors in the business. In this case, we were implementing during the pandemic. This meant that my team of over 100 consultants had to navigate a new virtual work environment, new relationships, and financial pressures. For these individuals, their physical environment was their home. But their virtual environment was an almost non-stop cadence of video meetings with stakeholders, leaders, partners, teams, etc. Furthermore, firm leadership was growing increasingly impatient, which resulted in tighter deadlines, less forgiveness for underperformance, and a churn in personnel. Of course, new team members only created more stress through increased onboarding, less familiarity, etc. This, in turn, increased the tension and frustration with senior leadership further. That created more meetings to review progress, more questions, less trust, and on and on. All of this dynamic could be felt, despite the team working remotely and spending very little time in person. This was our emotional environment. We were the walking embodiment of the phrase, "You could cut the tension with a knife." This was not psychological safety. While not quite toxic, it was definitely a sustained, negative environment.

It is important to acknowledge that safety is not equivalent to freedom from discomfort. In fact, quite the opposite. Psychological safety allows members of a group to understand that challenges will face them, but when they do face challenges, they will be supported. Too often, we remove the expectation of struggle. This is the criticism hurled at so-called "helicopter parents" who do everything for their children. So much so that their children grow up with real challenges in some key areas of life. As I'll share, how we define the experience of struggle and stress goes a long way to determining our individual and collective transformation success.

THE SOCIAL ENVIRONMENT

Our social environment plays another significant role in our ability to change. It goes without saying that humans are among the most social species on earth. Our ability to cooperate, along with our ability to communicate, are essential elements of our biological success. It is no surprise that our brains have evolved to ensure that this generally positive biological phenomenon continues. Historically, long before our modern existence, social interactions ensured critical elements of life— the ability to stay alive and the ability to find a mate. To ensure those things happened, the brain needed to create a mechanism that rewarded the social interaction behavior. That reward pathway starts at a brain region called the nucleus accumbens.

To summarize its function, the nucleus accumbens has a significant role in the cognitive processing of motivation, aversion, reward (i.e., incentive salience, pleasure, and positive reinforcement), and reinforcement learning. It's been long understood that the nucleus accumbens plays a role in virtually every reward experience we have as humans, from parent-child relationships to winning the lottery to addiction. Most significantly, the nucleus accumbens is an area rich with oxytocin receptors and that oxytocin is important in promoting sociability as a key behavior. When we interact in positive social experiences, oxytocin release in the nucleus accumbens then promotes the release of serotonin, which, as we learned in Chapter 1, plays a large role in how we experience emotions. Further research in 2022 then indicated that dopamine is also released from the nucleus accumbens during positive social interactions. In short, during social interactions, the nucleus accumbens becomes the epicenter of dopamine, oxytocin, and serotonin release in an intense hormonal cocktail. From a brain science perspective, social behaviors appear to be among the most important motivated human behaviors.

It is important to acknowledge that the circumstances and context of our modern world are now very different from what existed when our survival required living in groups for protection and procreation. Our modern lives allow for connections, both in person and not, of all types—from personal to professional to even anonymous. Our brains, however, still operate best through physical interaction with people with whom we have close social bonds. For example, social connectedness has been shown to decrease psychological and physiological deterioration. Studies in mice have shown that bystander mice develop pain symptomology simply by being in the presence of another mouse in pain. Similarly, a mouse in pain can experience analgesia (absence of pain) by being in the presence of a pain-free cohabitant. This happens through the connection between the nucleus accumbens and the anterior mid-cingulate cortex, that critical brain region we learned about in Chapter 1. Our brains were, in short, designed to be with other brains.

While it is generally true that our brains promote social interaction, it is important to understand that context matters. Without getting too technical (or at least more technical), the nucleus accumbens operates to both promote certain positive behaviors and intercept certain negative behaviors. For example, while we might make an off-color joke in front of family, we'd understand that at a professional dinner event that same joke might not be the best idea. While this may seem obvious, why does it matter in our experience of change? First, our interactions at work are only one small part of our human-to-human relationships. Second, the behaviors we are comfortable engaging in at work, or with work colleagues, are different than our behavior with closer social friends. Third, and most importantly, if we are asking people to change, primarily in the context of a professional experience, we are likely underleveraging the largest component of reward circuitry available to us in the experience of human change. In short, if we are relying only on professional, virtual relationships as motivation and reward for change, we will likely fall short of our expected goals.

In short, our environment and the quality of our relationship with the people that inhabit it with us are central to our ability to change. How we organize our environment to create constraints and access is critical toward our transformation journey. To do so, we have four environments we can shift: the physical, the virtual, the emotional, and the social. In many cases, shifting our physical environment requires that we remove options and create obstacles that embrace past behavior. This holds true for the virtual spaces in which we work. Our emotional environment, particularly at work, requires that we build a tone of psychological safety that allows others, and ourselves, to be free to transform. This is largely felt as the freedom to fail, to try, to experiment, and to learn. Finally, our social environment rests on the deep social connections we need as a species. We are, without question, underleveraging our social environment to create change. In each of these environments, small shifts can result in big changes.

CHAPTER 3

Strategy Two—
Initiate Movement

"The journey of a thousand miles begins with one step."
LAO TZU

QUITTERS DAY. EVER HEARD OF IT? It's January 19. That is the day, according to the fitness app Strava, that we give up on our New Year's Resolutions. By analyzing the data of over 800 app users, Strava determined that January 19th was the day most of us give up on our goals. Now, the good news is that we all can get started and maintain effortful progress for change for somewhere around 18 days, give or take. The bad news is that it doesn't take most of us long before we stop. Perhaps it's the string of early mornings at 5am to hit the gym before work that becomes too much. Perhaps it's the frustration of that new diet you've committed to that is so difficult to maintain. Maybe it's not having the time to practice that new language you thought you would learn. Or maybe that goal you had to finally learn piano. Every January millions upon millions of people aspire to change in some way. From accountability partners to vision boards (more on these later), for many of us, we are great at that initial first step toward change. There's excitement, energy, and enthusiasm. But, according to Strava, about three short weeks later, we stop.

The turn of the calendar is a visual signal for us. As we approach the end of every year and we take stock of our accomplishments, or setbacks, we envision a better future. Then we set goals for what we hope to achieve. Here's how it often goes. We indulge through the holidays while building a list of things we want to change. Be a better spouse. Be a better parent. Drink less. Sleep more. Read more. Eat healthier. Exercise. Among the litany of goals we identify, we select a few. Maybe we select them all. For now, let's just take at face value that most of us have a similar end-of-year conversation. As well as a start of the new year aspiration. All of it wrapped around our goals. Let's talk about those goals.

GOALS AND VISION

As a species, our visual sense is our most dominant sense. No other sense receives as much brain activity as our eyes. In fact, our eyes are our brains. They are the only portion of the brain that exists outside the skull. Of course, for those of us who lack sight, other senses play a critical role in their experience of the world. But for most of our history, vision has been the dominant sense with which we navigate the world.

It stands to reason then that when we think about goals, our vision plays a critical role. From goal setting to goal pursuit, our vision is central to generating the motivation needed to accomplish our objectives. We've all visualized in our "mind's eye," an inspiring future we want to achieve. We've laid out that visual roadmap of all the activities and milestones needed to transform our organization. The visual representation of not just this new future, but also the path to get there, is how we not only organize our minds, but how we generate the initial motivation to act.

However, we also know our vision is imperfect and that if anything stays in our visual field for too long, it can fade into the background. Like those sticky notes on the wall, or that vision board you built, or your grandmother's wallpaper from the 80s, we stop seeing things that are always present. That same roadmap that is so initially motivating becomes a daunting plan with too many steps over too long a timeframe to keep our motivation high. It's the transformational equivalent of "our mouths are bigger than our stomach."

There's good news, however. According to Dr. Emily Balcetis, we can work with, perhaps even manipulate, the gap between our visual perception and reality. In her book, *Clearer, Closer, Better,* Dr. Balcetis' research highlights an important attribute of the visual—goal relationship: when we narrow our visual focus, we increase our chances of reaching our goals. For example, in the multi-step, multi-year transformation roadmap, if we look at the whole picture, we struggle to take the next step. But when we can focus on the next step, we are much more likely to make progress. In research of high-performance athletes, it was found that this narrowing of visual focus was a common strategy in achieving goals. Turns out this works for average, everyday people as well. In a study performed by Hal Hershfield, he found that showing people a visual image of themselves in retirement forty-five years into the future increased the amount of money they saved daily compared to those who only saw current photos of themselves. Like a marathon runner who focuses on the next mile instead of mile twenty-six, the nearer our goals the more likely we are to generate the motivation and effort to pursue them.

This raises an important point about the nature of goals themselves. In the research noted above, participants were moving towards a goal. This is what's called an Approach Goal. Another type of goal is an Avoidance Goal. Or something you want to move away from. Many of our New Year's resolutions take the form of avoidance goals: eat less junk food, lose twenty pounds, and so on. Some goals, such as reading more, sleeping more, or being a better spouse, are approach goals in intent, although our motivation for them is often a function of some avoidance behavior at its core. For example, if I want to sleep more, then I need to watch less TV or scroll less on social media. It turns out that the manner in which we frame or define our goals plays a critical role in our motivation to pursue them. At least initially. Dr. Maya Shankar has done extensive research on this topic.

It also matters *who* defines our goals. When we define goals for ourselves, we are far more motivated to pursue them. Decades of research on student behaviors, for example, concludes that providing students with choices leads to increased autonomy and, in turn, motivation and learning. In short, when we get to design our goals, we are far more attached to them than when they are handed to us by others.

THE SCIENCE OF GOAL MOTIVATION

The science of goal motivation traces back to the early 1930s, 40s and 50s, with research into animal behavior and has since launched countless human studies, such as those highlighted by Dr. Balcetis. The foundational research into goal pursuit was done by Clark L. Hull. Hull developed the goal gradient hypothesis, which states that motivation to accomplish a goal increases monotonically from the goal initiation state to the goal ending state. The closer we get to the end of a goal pursuit, the harder we work. This is true even when we are in states of energy deprivation. When combined with our understanding of visual motivational cues, when we can see the end in sight, our brains trigger the release of dopamine, and we work harder to finish. A narrow focus on a close-in goal is the key to generating motivation.

Let's return briefly to an important neuroscience concept introduced previously—our brains are prediction machines, and they form predictions based on our experience. Hull's work showed that as we get close to the end of a goal, we will exert increasing levels of effort. What's been proven since, however, is that our perception of the difficulty of that goal significantly influences our willingness to exert effort in the first place. A 2007 study indicated that mental fatigue affects the anterior mid-cingulate cortex [aMCC]—that critical brain region that controls just about everything we do. A range of additional studies have shown two critical resulting effects. One, mental fatigue impacts physical and cognitive performance. This is unsurprising. Two, and potentially more importantly, our perception of the effort required to achieve a goal directly correlates with our willingness to exert effort in the first place. When the world looks difficult, complex, and challenging, we are less likely to put in the effort required. It's a vicious circle and one that, for people with various chronic conditions, can lead to a spiral. Goals seem farther away. Hills seem steeper. Life gets heavier. If the story your brain is telling you is that "this will never work" or "I can't do it," the ripple effects into your ability to provide the effort to pursue a goal, let alone to get started, is significant.

In the world of change and transformation, it's clear why this matters. For every person who can look at that multi-year roadmap and see the next step clearly and with motivation, there's a person who sees the totality of this giant plan and is paralyzed. For every person who is motivated by doing something hard, there is a person whose brain tells them there's no reason to start because "this will fail like every other past initiative." The answer to this challenge of hesitation is often the creation of inspiring visions of the future. Instead of focusing on the plan, we tell people to focus on what their new reality will be like when it's all said and done. One of the en vogue methods for doing this is vision boards (I told you we were going to talk about this).

While there are variations to vision boards, the concept behind a vision board is to create visual representations of your life after a change has taken place. These images are designed to motivate you to act, to go get the thing on the board. It turns out, much to the chagrin of Instagram's gurus, that it doesn't work. In fact, it does the opposite. Positive fantasies allow people to mentally indulge in a desired future and, in doing so, this lowers their systolic blood pressure, which is a key signal for action within the body. When we indulge mentally in our desired future state, we experience enough of it cognitively such that we become less motivated to take any additional action. Remember that visual cues are important for our willingness to pursue a goal. But too much of a good thing can backfire. We either lose sight of the goal as our visual cues fade into the background or our brain decides that we've already achieved the goal, so there's no reason to start.

GETTING STARTED

The question that stands before us now is *how do we put this insight into practice*? We know we need a visual connection to pursue our goals. But we can't overdo it with so many visuals that we lower systolic blood pressure and reduce motivation. We know we have increased motivation to finish a goal that is close to being complete but, depending on the perception of our brain, we may never get started in the first place. We know that when we start, we have about three weeks of motivation, give or take, before the Quitters Day phenomenon creeps in. We also know that Approach Goals are more motivating than Avoidance Goals. Yet, much of our goal structure begins with avoidance incentives.

This section is about initiating movement. While it's easy to say "just do it" the preceding content makes it clear we need a little more than that. With that, here are four steps we can take to initiate movement.

Step 1: Define an Approach Goal

Shifting from Avoidance to Approach Goals is the first place to start. An easy version of this shift is to reframe the goal of losing twenty pounds, to one of living a healthy lifestyle. An organizational example might be shifting from the goal of cutting fifty million dollars to becoming an efficient, high-profit company. In each case, while the original incentive might have been to lose something—weight or operating costs respectively—there is a larger, more motivating goal that we actually want to attain.

Step 2: Reframe the Start

We must define getting started as a goal in and of itself. For a marathon runner, their first goal of the day is to wake up on time. The second is to conduct their pre-race morning routine. The third is to get to the race location and warm up. By the time the gun is fired, they have accomplished three, if not more, things. Redefining starting as the end of the beginning helps us narrow our focus towards the initial experience.

Some may consider this a bit of a mental game equivalent to setting your clock ten minutes ahead to trick yourself into waking up on time. If you know the clock is ten minutes off, you're only going to give yourself an extra ten minutes before you get out of bed. Recall two important details about your brain. First, as humans, our perception of difficulty influences our experience of difficulty. Second, when we do hard things, our anterior mid-cingulate cortex [aMCC] learns to view other hard things as, quite simply, less difficult.

Step 3: Reframe your Mental Model

Along with reframing goals, we must reframe our mental model. One way to think of this is to simply stop listening to your inner narrative or fear signals. If we understand that our brain can only reference our own experiences to make future predictions, we can intercept that process. Or at least ignore it. For example, if you've historically been someone who never finishes what you start, you are also someone who is successful at starting new things. Yes, the Quitters Day effect is a real thing. But you can only quit something you've already started. This reframing could easily be modified to think about change as a sequence of starting points linked together over time. When I do that, I can leverage my successes to keep performing consistently. Instead of seeing that multi-year roadmap as a slog of endless, integrated activities, I can see the series of individual starting points and orient my goal completion there. Carol Dweck would call this *growth mindset* in action.

Step 4: Manage the Messy Middle

By reframing change as a series of goals, we can better manage the messy middle of goal pursuit. To use the marathon analogy again, runners will often find other runners in the crowd who they want to pass. As they get close, the goal-gradient effect kicks in. When they pass them, they will find the next runner, set a new goal, and start the process again.

Let me give you an example from my life. I use a similar process during my weekly one-hour run. Since I don't have other runners to visually align with, I use time. My first goal is the start and initial five minutes. I'm simply performing one five-minute run. My next goal is to the twenty-minute mark, which is simply another fifteen-minute run. The next goal is to do one half of what I already completed. Or a ten-minute run. This takes me to fifty-percent completion. Once I've reached the halfway point, I only need one more ten-minute run to complete two-thirds, or sixty-six percent, of my hour. It's at this point that I shift my focus. Instead of focusing on one twenty-minute run, I narrow the goal to four five-minute runs. I also increase my speed. The goal gradient effect is taking over. The last mile of my weekly run is often my fastest, despite the fact that I've already run four-ish miles by that point. By getting started, and having a plan for the middle, I am able to get close enough to the finish line that my brain releases more dopamine, and I get a boost of energy.

Step 5: Strategize Obstacles

One of the contributors to the Quitters Day effect is our struggle to forecast all the ways pursuing one's goal could go wrong. We must be careful here. In reframing our mental model, it is easy to get into failure-based thinking that deters us from starting. Strategizing obstacles is different. It's a game plan for what you're going to do when circumstances change. If my Approach Goal is to eat healthier, then I need to have a plan for when I'm out to eat, or when my spouse makes chocolate chip cookies, or when I'm traveling for work. It turns out, by the way, that strategizing alternatives leverages the same vision-motivation link. But unlike a vision board that lowers systolic blood pressure, because I'm focusing on the end state of my goal, envisioning alternatives emphasizes the actions I can take to stay in goal-pursuit mode. Even if those circumstances do not occur, visualizing alternatives is a key component for how we can reframe and retrain our aMCC as well.

A famous example of this strategy in action is Michael Phelps, the most accomplished swimmer in history. In 2008, while performing the 200m butterfly, Phelps' goggles filled up with water twenty-five meters into the race. In the run-up to the Olympics, Phelps had practiced for this scenario by training to count his strokes. He knew exactly the number of strokes he needed to take with each leg. As his goggles filled up, he switched to counting strokes and won the gold. Sports teams, military teams, first responders—all understand that scenario planning is key to maintaining motivation and performance. Strategizing obstacles is akin to following the wise advice of then General Dwight D. Eisenhower during World War: "Plans are useless, but planning is indispensable."

Step 6: Leverage Groups for Motivation

As we've learned, positive social interaction is among the most neurologically rewarding behaviors we can engage in. It stands to reason then, that we should leverage groups to initiate and maintain movement.

Strategies for Regulating Motivation

Underlying the ability to initiate movement towards our goals is the ability to generate the motivation to act. In the sections above, we've explored how our approach toward framing and pursuing goals can work with, or against, our biology. In addition to reframing our approach to goals, we can also improve our own ability to generate the dopamine needed to get moving. After all, it's a requirement for goal pursuit. Or, as Dr. Anna Lembke, a professor of psychiatry and behavioral sciences and the chief of the Addiction Medicine Dual Diagnosis Clinic at Stanford, said, "Dopamine is about wanting, not about having."

The following are ways to improve your baseline levels of dopamine to increase your chances of initiating movement. When matched with the goal strategies above, we significantly increase our likelihood of initiating and maintaining movement by:

- Viewing early morning sunlight for 10–30 minutes daily.

- Take a 1–3-minute cold shower, as cold as you can safely tolerate.

- Eat tyrosine-rich foods such as red meats, nuts, or hard fermented cheese.

- Avoid melatonin supplements, as these can decrease dopamine levels and can disrupt your normal sleep patterns.

- Avoid viewing bright lights between 10 p.m. – 4 a.m.

- Ingest caffeine (approximately 100–400mg) in the form of coffee, tea, or whatever form you prefer.

- Use (randomly) Intermittent Reward Timing (RIRT) to celebrate your wins, but do not celebrate every win. When you succeed in reaching a milestone, sometimes enjoy that; at other times (at random), just keep going.

- Incorporate spotlighting (as discussed in the section on narrowing our visual focus).

Successful transformation relies heavily on effectively directing our visual system and method for goal framing in a manner that works with our natural motivation systems. When we can narrow our focus on an initial set of near-term goals and build strategies that will maintain our motivation to act, we are able to link together behaviors that result in real change. However, we must understand that the same vision that helps us act is the same vision that can overwhelm our motivational sensors. By reframing, not only how we define our goals, but our inner narrative around the complexity of the challenges in front of us, we can retrain our brain to move past the initial hurdles of getting started so we can benefit from the natural dopamine effect that occurs as we move closer to completing our goals. By leveraging individual strategies for dopamine regulation in concert with smaller, incremental goals, we can successfully navigate the messy middle of change and transformation.

CHAPTER 4

Strategy Three—
Embrace Stress

"Stress is simply the adaptation
of our bodies and minds to change."
PETER G. HANSON, M.D.

O N MARCH 20, 1998, military forces from the former Yugoslavia began an operation to expel the Kosovo Liberation Army from Kosovo, a small territory at the southern end of the Balkans. One month prior to that, as a new junior intelligence officer at the Defense Intelligence Agency, I was selected for a rotational assignment in the Pentagon to serve as the "senior" air defense analyst to the Joint Chiefs of Staff. My role was to help the US military understand and prepare for a possible military conflict as part of its peacekeeping role as a member of the North Atlantic Treaty Organization (NATO). In this position, I led a team of twelve military and civilian intelligence officers to compile a comprehensive understanding of air-defense operations in the region and provide this information to US policymakers and military leaders. Beginning on March 24, the day the US air strikes began, I worked ninety-two days straight, from 4 a.m. to 8 p.m. It was a daily, non-stop, high-pressure experience. While I wasn't at what we call the "pointy end of the spear", I was part of a complex network of military operations that culminated in the withdrawal of Yugoslav forces from the region. To this day, it remains one of the most formative experiences of my life.

How did a twenty-five-year-old, know-nothing, junior analyst get such a job, you might ask? Well, I raised my hand. That's right. I simply said, "I'll do it." Ironically, there was a senior analyst who had been studying the region for nearly twenty years who would have been the more logical choice. He had the experience, expertise, and history of the region. But he didn't want to work nights and weekends. So, it appeared that my only real qualifications at that point were youth and stamina. Never underestimate the value of perseverance.

While I have many memories from this experience, the most important of which is simply the sheer magnitude of real military operations, I remember March 25 like it was yesterday. The day prior, NATO began air strikes in the region. As was my role, I was monitoring the results of the air strikes, analyzing movements of our adversary, synthesizing other sources of intelligence, and preparing for the next round of strikes. It was around 7pm at the Pentagon and I received a call from my task force leader. "Hey, Lopez. They want to see you upstairs."

"Who's they?" I asked.

"Don't know. Just head up to the 5th floor."

This is where most of the senior leaders are.

I had been at the Pentagon for nearly thirty-six hours by this point. While operating on a fair bit of adrenaline still, I was tired. But this call snapped me into immediate focus. I grabbed some of my notes and headed upstairs. I arrived on the fifth floor and headed into the conference room. As I walked into the room, I was immediately struck by the audience. Sitting in front of me was probably 1,000 years of combined military experience. A room of twenty or so people, punctuated by the Chief of Staff of the Air Force, four two-and-three-star generals and admirals, several "full bird" colonels, two representatives from the US House of

Representatives, the chair of the Senate Armed Services Committee, a litany of other senior civilians and staffers . . . and me. Twenty-five-year-old "senior" air defense analyst me. "Have a seat," I hear from the two-star Air Force General responsible for air operations. Sweating at that point, I sat. "Tell us what happened today," he said.

Upon sitting, I felt my heart racing. As I started to talk, my voice cracked. A surge of cortisol (which I didn't know at the time) triggered the release of epinephrine, which created the secondary effect of dilating my blood vessels rapidly. Blood moved from my arms and legs into my chest to protect my vital organs. Sweat pooled under my arms due to the increased heart rate and slight elevation of body temperature. My visual field narrowed dramatically. I could no longer see the entire room, only the general who asked me the initial question. I answered. Then a different general tossed another question at me. My visual field shifted to him. I had nearly forgotten the previous question because I was intently focused on the next. With each question and answer, I became slightly more relaxed. By the end of the meeting, I was far more comfortable with the conversation. My heart rate had slowed. I was sweating less. I could see the larger room. I was alert and focused, but not overwhelmed.

Welcome to the world of stress.

I share this story to illustrate two dimensions of stress. First, while my life certainly wasn't threatened at that moment, it reacted in the same manner as if threatened. My body simply reacted. My brain, upon entering this room full of very senior, important people, made several predictions about what would happen next. Remember, our brains are prediction machines. It then began the almost instantaneous process of assigning resources to my body in the form of a stress response. I experienced this, and the subsequent bodily responses, as an intense form of stress. Second, and most importantly, how I responded to that stress was a function of the decisions I made well in advance of it. As an athlete, I had put myself in several stressful situations. I was familiar with the stress response. In the month before the air campaign started, I had also had time to learn, fail, prepare, and grow. While the moment itself was an entirely new experience, particularly for someone my age,

I could call upon stressful experiences in my past. What resulted was still the physical experience of stress, but stress directed at improving my performance. Increased alertness, greater focus, reduced sensations in non-essential elements of my body. All of these were the productive result of channeling short-term stress. Don't get me wrong, I was terrified. But, because I had done hard things in my past, my brain, while still predicting stress, was able to pull from other positive experiences with stress, which allowed me to perform. In short, while it was my first time being in this stressful situation, it wasn't my first time being stressed. And that matters.

There's another element of stress worth noting from this experience— adaptation. What you don't know yet is how the story ended. For ninety-one days after that first stressful meeting, I worked in this intensely high-pressure situation. While difficult, I became accustomed to the pace and intensity of the work. I adapted. I adapted so much that when the war ended and I returned to my regular job, I wasn't the same. Being an intelligence analyst is a lot like being a journalist. Imagine going from reporting on the front lines of a battle to returning home and doing a long-term study. It's a stark contrast. I couldn't focus without the hustle and bustle of the twenty-four-hour military cycle. What's more, at that pace, my health suffered. I wasn't sleeping well. My relationships were negatively affected. So, while I might have raised my threshold for managing high stress, the prolonged experience had other deleterious outcomes.

WHAT IS STRESS?

The word stress was popularized by Dr. Selye, who defined it as "the non-specific response of the body to any demand for change." The experience of how we adapt to the phases of stress is termed the General Adaptation Syndrome (GAS), a term coined by Dr. Selye. More recently, in medicine, stress is best understood as "the body's response to physical, mental, or emotional pressure." In this sense, we can understand stress as a more generic system that is used to mobilize other systems in the body. As a generic system, it operates like an on-off switch. So, whether you're being chased by the sabertoothed tiger or standing in a meeting in the

Pentagon, your brain and body create a stress response. As we'll come to learn, it is a system hardwired into our bodies that was not designed for just one event. In fact, when we think about the fact that bones and muscles grow when under stress, that we learn more from failure than success (more on this later), we can come to understand a fundamental truth about humans and stress—the human body was designed to understand stress. More importantly, it was designed to perform under stress. This may sound somewhat heretical in this day and age, but it is absolutely true.

Let's dive into the physiology of stress. The stress response operates like a cascade that begins in the amygdala, which signals the hypothalamus, which communicates with the rest of the body through the sympathetic nervous system and the parasympathetic nervous systems. The sympathetic nervous system functions like a gas pedal in a car. It triggers the fight-or-flight response, providing the body with a burst of energy so it can respond to perceived dangers. The parasympathetic nervous system acts like a brake.

Within the sympathetic nervous system are a group of neurons that start at your neck and run down your spine to about your navel. This is called the sympathetic chain ganglia. When we encounter a stress trigger, that set of neurons reacts like a bunch of dominoes falling. When that happens, those neurons release acetylcholine into our muscles, which sends the signal for us to move. A secondary set of neurons then creates epinephrine—or adrenaline. That epinephrine acts in three ways: 1) it dilates the blood vessels and moves blood into things we need, like the heart, lungs, legs, brain, 2) it releases cortisol and glucose to augment energy reserves, and 3) it signals other, less critical systems—such as digestion, reproduction—to shut down as those are not needed in the current, stressful situation. This is what I experienced when I walked into that March 25, 1998 meeting and what you experience when someone cuts you off on the road. The wiring for this process is so efficient that it starts well before we are often even conscious of it. Remember, we are prediction machines. It's why if someone shouts, "LOOK OUT!" In almost any circumstance, we will react. We don't even yet know what we're looking out for. We just react.

The longer the brain perceives the threat stimulus, the longer this process continues, the more cortisol is released into the body. When the threat passes, the parasympathetic nervous system takes over, applies the "brake" in our physiological response, and cortisol levels fall.

This is a good point to mention something important about stress. In the short term, stress is incredibly beneficial. The stress response is, at its core, the mobilization of our body's resources to get us to act. Remember my meeting at the Pentagon? The stress response allowed me to focus intensely to ensure I was sharing the right information at the right time with the right people. As we learned in Chapter 3, initiating movement toward our goals requires that we marshal resources and focus. In the short-term, the release of cortisol creates important immune-protective effects within the body. The same system that is used to avoid cars while walking across the street is the same system that is used to fight bacteria or viral infection at the microscopic level within the body. Again, one system, multiple purposes.

This is a good point to revisit the General Adaptation Syndrome published by Hans Selye. What was just described as the short-term stress response is what Dr. Selye calls the "Alarm Reaction Stage." In this case, short-term is defined as the initial trigger event and subsequent stress response. After this initial trigger event and stress response comes the "Resistance Stage." In this stage, the body begins to repair itself from the stress event. Although your body enters this recovery phase, it remains on high alert for a while. If you overcome stress and the situation is no longer an issue, your body continues to repair itself until your hormone levels, heart rate, and blood pressure reach a pre-stress state. If the stress does not resolve itself, your body adapts to more persistent levels of stress. To do so, your body maintains a state of semi-stress induced response, such elevated blood pressure, persistently high cortisol, and increased glucose levels. Persisting in this phase leads to the final stage, "Exhaustion." In this phase, we no longer have the resources to productively respond to stress. Fatigue, poor concentration, poor sleep, limited physical recovery, happen here. This can lead to burnout, depression, as well as a litany of other physical ailments, such as lack of sleep and inflammation.

If short-term stress is good, long-term stress is bad. The challenge, of course, is understanding when that cut-off point is. What is considered long-term can vary from person to person. More importantly, even medium-term stress, without proper strategies to resolve it, can be quite damaging. Much like my experience in the Pentagon, while that initial meeting was ultimately a growth experience, it's clear that ninety-two-straight days of working in that environment crossed the medium to long-term threshold. Herein lies the question that we all must ask ourselves on the journey to transformation—how might we harness the benefits of short-term stress to create the movement we need towards our goals, without tripping into the negative effects caused from prolonged, unresolved stress?

RETHINKING OUR RELATIONSHIP WITH STRESS

Without question, there are real, significant stressors that, unfortunately, impact many people daily. We understand the debilitating effects of long-term stress on people, particularly children. In many cases, systemic or structural factors create stress that sits outside of our, or their, control. At the same time, I believe the concept of all stress as bad holds us back. Like it or not, stress is an enduring reality of the human experience. If we are to be successful in change, we must change our relationship to stress. We must shift from building strategies to avoid the discomfort of stress to embracing the benefits of short-term stress. We must move from passenger to driver. While we cannot consciously control the physiological stress response, we can dramatically improve our relationship with it. So much so that we can effectively aim it at the goals we desire most.

The first step in rethinking our relationship to stress involves what we've already covered—understanding the mechanisms themselves. This is important because when we understand what's happening under the hood—to extend the car analogy—we are less mystified by the experience. Look, no one said the stress response is pleasant. It can be intensely uncomfortable. But it's just another prediction from the brain. Whether it's sweaty palms on a first date or butterflies before a speech to the class, our body is simply priming itself for the moment. When

I have this sensation, I'm reminded of one of my favorite quotes from my high school coach who said, "You can't get the butterflies in your stomach to go away. But, you can get them to fly in formation.".

The second step in rethinking our relationship to stress is to induce it. All too often, the stress we experience is a function of things that happen to us because of interactions with others. It's rarely the thing we've done to ourselves. Recall that in Chapter 1 we explored how this critical brain region called the Anterior Mid-Cingulate Cortex gets bigger when we do hard things. When we create stress by choosing to induce it ourselves, two things happen. First, we learn to experience the intensity of the experience less. And two, we get better at dealing with other stressful events in the future.

This makes perfect sense when we think about physical performance, yet we don't apply the same principles to our behavior. We understand that to make a muscle stronger we must put that muscle under tension, increasing degrees of tension over time. We don't go for a ten-mile run the first time we jog. We build up to that experience. And yet, when it comes to behaviors, we just expect people to "get it" the first time. Research by James McGaugh has demonstrated that, for example, memory performance follows an inverted U-shaped relationship. At two ends of the stress spectrum, i.e., too little, or too much, mental performance suffers. At the midpoint of this spectrum, working memory is improved. Just like it is with a muscle, just the right amount of stress is required for mental performance. We allow for a proper warmup before exercise or before that championship game. But we want just enough of a warmup to not fatigue the body. We need to be in the sweet spot. It turns out non-physical performance works in the same way.

While any uncomfortable activity can induce stress, two strategies have been shown to be particularly effective based on scientific research. One is cold water immersion. Be it a cold plunge or cold shower, cold water is an extremely effective stress-inducing mechanism. Cold water immersion triggers rapid breathing and stimulates the adrenal glands to release adrenaline, which we know is in the cascade chain of the stress response. The second, which can be done without cold water, is a rapid breathing protocol similar to what would happen if you were immersed in cold water. Rapid breathing, performed in quick inhales and exhales (twenty to twenty-five reps) followed by a fifteen-second breath hold, creates a similar adrenal gland response. It's important to do these in a safe location (e.g. not in water) as it can create a hyperventilation effect. But with the proper training, this style of breathing is tremendously effective in simulating a stress response for your body.

The third step in rethinking our relationship with stress is reframing our understanding of the emotions that come with it. As we learned, our emotions are a function of how accurate our brain is at predicting what will happen next. Things like frustration, anger, and disappointment, among others, are all the result when things don't go our way. If we can reframe both our expectations and our understanding of the emotions that result when we venture into those territories, we can better withstand the stress that comes with them. This is not a commercial for adopting some kind of Zen, nihilistic, stoic mentality where nothing matters. It's a reminder that just because our bodies are experiencing stress, we do not need to automatically associate that sensation with negative emotions. This, in my opinion, is at the root of Quitters Day. In pursuing our new goals, we find out that it's stressful to change. That stress turns into discomfort, which turns into frustration. And with enough sustained frustration, we simply stop the pursuit.

Which leads us to the final element of rethinking our relationship to stress: our beliefs about stress itself. Here, we return to the brief discussion introduced in Chapter 1 about a growth mindset as well as a stress-is-enhancing mindset. In 2013, Drs. Dweck and Crum demonstrated three critical findings. First, the extent to which an individual believes stress is either debilitating or enhancing has a direct impact on their somatic experience of that stress. Second, that core mindset can be altered through relatively simple education and training. Third, a stress-is-enhancing mindset is associated with moderate cortisol reactivity, e.g., shorter duration of cortisol release.

More recently, the work of David Yaeger furthered our understanding by performing studies of the synergistic effects of training both a growth and stress-is-enhancing mindset together. Through a great paper titled *A synergistic mindsets intervention protects adolescents from stress* published in *Nature* in 2022, Yaeger and his colleagues demonstrated that when students are taught about growth mindset and a stress-is-enhancing mindset, they perform much better in stressful situations. Furthermore, when students apply multiple mindsets in anticipation of a stressful experience, they have a greater buffer in the physiological experience of that stress. And, as a result, improved performance. This training was performed in a thirty-minute online video training. In short, a little positive thinking about stress goes a long way.

When it comes to the experience of stress, we know more than ever before. While it's easy to understand stress as the early physiological response to danger and survival, the stress response serves many important purposes in our lives. Its principal function is to mobilize us to move towards or away from something. Anything. In that regard, stress is a critical human function and, as stated, provides important short-term benefits to multiple dimensions of our growth. No one is saying that stress will feel good. Nor are we suggesting that stress will always lead to better performance. Stress, in and of itself, is neither good nor bad. We simply understand stress as a pre-requisite for human growth and transformation.

To successfully change, we must rethink and embrace our relationship with stress. The more we can place ourselves in safe but adaptive stress situations and shift our mind away from the raw, uncomfortable experience of it, the more we can benefit from the positive physiological effects of stress. In doing so, we shift our focus away from the somatic, physical experience of stress, and allow ourselves to understand why we are experiencing the stress. This is possible when we adopt and apply both a growth and stress-is-enhancing mindset. The synergistic effect of this increased awareness is felt physiologically in the form of lower cortisol released, improved blood flow during stressful situations, and other benefits, as well as in our ability to perform under conditions of stress.

Our path through change requires that we rebuild our relationship with stress and embrace its positive, short-term effects. Cold showers, breathwork, and intense physical exercise are strategies we can use to increase our experience of stress in the short-term, as well as raise our stress thresholds in the medium- term. When combined with the foundations of positive health, from sleep, to nutrition, to regular exercise, we stand to harness stress' positive outcomes in an array of change experiences. However, long-term stress remains one of the most health and performance damaging experiences one can sustain. In these circumstances, receiving clinical support is critical. In addition, leveraging the power of our social structures and relationships is a critical long-term stress buffer. After all, as previously shared, pro-social interactions are among the most biologically rewarding behaviors we can engage in. Quite simply, our ability to embrace and withstand this very necessary human experience we call stress is essential if we are to successfully change.

CHAPTER 5

Strategy Four— Create Focus

"You must unlearn what you have learned."
JEDI MASTER YODA

A S I WRITE THIS CHAPTER, my wife is about two weeks away from giving birth to our daughter. It's an incredibly exciting time for us. As we prepare for our new arrival, I'm reminded that babies give us our earliest look into the human nervous system. But not always in the ways people expect. While we all understand that babies lack refined movement, detailed vision, language, and so on, it's natural to think that this is because their nervous systems are underdeveloped. However, they are, in fact, overdeveloped. What this means is that the early nervous system is a hyperconnected web of neurons that have not yet created established patterns. It's like a set of roads all leading in different directions with no rhyme or reason to their beginning or end. While my daughter has been slowly growing, her body has been prioritizing the development of the autonomic nervous system, the system that controls those largely unconscious and critical functions that keep us alive—everything from maintaining our heartbeat, to breathing, to regulating hormones. You might recognize this from Chapter 1 and the work of Dr. Feldman Barrett as the brain's principal responsibility to manage our body budget, which is the assignment of bodily resources to our most critical functions. This makes complete sense, given that she will enter this big new world, and her body needs to prioritize the most basic functions of survival.

Her somatic nervous system—which is associated with the voluntary control of body movements via skeletal muscles—however, is quite the opposite. Her somatic nervous system is like a jumbled connection of neurons with no real pattern. It's much like a map of ancient Rome with many small roads, all leading in different directions without any discernible pattern. This highly connected, in fact over-connected, network represents an endless number of future possible nervous system patterns that will emerge over the first few critical years of life. What establishes the more refined pattern? Experience, of course. But what experience does is quite interesting: it strips away the neural connections we don't need. In the analogy of ancient Rome, we simply stop using that small road that leads to one place in favor of another road. Over time, the path we've traveled becomes familiar. We stop maintaining the other road. It falls into disrepair. And is eventually replaced by something else. This is why my daughter already "knows" the sound of mommy's and daddy's voice at birth. It's not that she actually knows who we are. It's that her neurons have created a stronger pathway towards a repetitive, familiar sound that, when she's out of the womb and in the world, she will recognize.

This process of stripping away unused connections and prioritizing others is the basis for how our brains develop. In the early years of childhood, we make more neurons than at any point in our lives. As they form, they enter this hyper-connected patchwork. Small unorganized roads give way to more established superhighways of connectivity. The more we take a certain action, the stronger that highway gets. The less we take an action, the farther into disrepair the road falls. For example, my son, who is now sixteen years old, started out life left-handed. Starting at around ten-months old, he clearly demonstrated a preference for this hand. Then, right around fourteen-months-old, he decided to jump off the couch (because why not) and as he fell, he put that preferred left arm out to support his fall. And he broke it. Well, more like bent it. Because baby bones are softer, they bend. And because they bend, babies usually spend longer in a cast to ensure the bone and growth plates do not suffer any long-term distortion. So, my son spent the next twelve weeks with a cast on his preferred left arm. Within that span, he shifted to his right hand. But something interesting occurred. While he lost some of the preference on his left side, he remains ambidextrous. At sixteen, he's an incredible high school quarterback with his right arm and an amazing baseball pitcher. But he bats left-handed. While he can't throw with his left hand to the same degree he now can with his right, he has retained some of that left-handed pathway originally established.

THE SCIENCE OF CHANGING YOUR NERVOUS SYSTEM

Our understanding of the nervous system is, in modern science, a relatively recent phenomenon. In the late 1950s, David Hubel and Torsten Wiesel started their journey as the godfathers of understanding the visual system and, by extension, the nervous system. The entire basis of neuroplasticity is based on their incredibly groundbreaking work. Their work focused on how limitations in the visual system for young children would result in the brain re-wiring itself to accommodate the visual limitations. In effect, they proved how my son's brain would eventually re-wire itself to account for his broken arm. While this seems like common knowledge today, their work would create the foundation for what we understand as neuroplasticity today. Their work represented a quantum leap in science and would win them the Nobel Prize.

We are all born with a nervous system that is designed to change. And that change is possible throughout our entire life. We can think about this change experience in phases. In the early years of life, we experience what's called, according to Dr. Mike Merzenich at the University of California at San Francisco, the critical period. In this period, our brain is at the mercy of our environment. We are absorbing information and experience with little effort on our part. In these early years, we are building more neurons than at any other point in our life, and the neural pathways that are established create a critical foundation for who we become as people. It's one reason why early life trauma can be such a challenging and damaging experience as we grow older. Even single, emotionally intense or stressful events create what are called "one trial learning" experiences that can have long-lasting effects on neural pathways. We continue this process of creating new neurons roughly through puberty.

The second phase runs from puberty to roughly twenty-five (not a hard limit), where the creation of new neurons slows and the process of removing neural pathways continues. With the slowing of new neurons, we see the early signs of the adult brain, though we understand that in this phase, the frontal lobe remains largely undeveloped. Behavior becomes engrained through repetition (this is called long-term potentiation, which we'll talk more about in Chapter 6) and pathways for behavior we no longer engage in weaken (called long-term depression).

The final phase, according to Dr. Merzenich, is adult plasticity. By this point, your nervous system is a customized map of your individual life experience. And, as we learned in Chapter 1, your brain is making instantaneous predictions of the future according to your unique brain map. Those predictions are so embedded into your nervous system that your body reacts instantly and unconsciously, creating everything from your perceptions, to your emotions, to your actions. What's unique about Dr. Merzenich's description of adult plasticity is that adult plasticity requires what he calls "attentional control."

It's at this point that we must engage in a completely different set of behaviors in order to change. One, we aren't creating new neurons that can be directed toward new actions. This means we must use the neurons we have. Two, this requires that we re-purpose existing pathways to new behaviors. And three, to do so, we must decide which behaviors we want to give up, or not engage in, so we can make space for new actions. In short, learning becomes a bit of a zero-sum game. Herein lies the challenge. Giving up the thing that we already know how to do is difficult. It's stressful. It's inefficient. Learning does not just happen because we are exposed to something new. It happens because we intensely focus on a new action. And, more importantly, we decide—

intentionally or otherwise—what we will NOT do to make space. Our ability to learn is not governed by whether we *can* learn, it's governed by whether we *believe* we have something to learn. In short, we must focus. We must dedicate attentional control. What is attentional control? It is, put simply, focus.

FOUNDATIONS OF FOCUS AND NERVOUS SYSTEM CHANGE

It's important that we dispel a myth before we go any further. That myth is that every experience you have changes your brain. This is not true unless you are a young child. You might be thinking, "But Michael, you said our brains are a unique map of our experience." This is true. Your brain is a map of your experience up to that point in your life. However, one new experience—unless it's a highly emotional, intense experience—doesn't change that map. We no longer learn through environmental exposure as we once did in that critical first period of life. This is where we struggle.

The first step in changing your brain is to recognize that you want to change something. We don't have to be overly specific about what that change looks like. We simply need to identify some specific aspect of our behavior that we want to shift. This could be learning a language, or playing pickleball, or being more patient with our children. When we identify a behavior we desire to shift, we generally do so in the form of a goal. As discussed, goals can be either defined as something we want to move toward, an approach goal, or something that we want to avoid, an avoidance goal. In this case, we must move the goal beyond the abstract and create a more specific intention of the goal we are pursuing. For example, I don't just want to learn piano. I want to learn piano at this specific moment. I don't just want to learn to be patient. I want to be patient at this specific moment.

This is not some murky concept. When we have an intentional, narrow focus, we signal to our brain that the thing we are focusing on is important enough to pay attention to. This is the foundation of adult learning. Language is a simple example. As children, simple exposure to multiple languages rapidly accelerates their ability to speak multiple languages. So much so that learning new languages later in life can be easier for them. After all, they have established the neural pathways for language adoption. But for adults who grew up in a single language household, learning a new language requires focused intervals of intense practice. We must dedicate ourselves to the practice of learning the language.

When we bring intentional focus to learning, we cue the brain to release two important neurochemicals necessary to move the brain from a desire to change to actual change. The first is epinephrine. That's right, the same hormone involved in the early stages of the stress response. This is why we must change our relationship to stress if we want to change. When we draw our attention to an important moment that is in line with our change objectives, the brain releases epinephrine. It does so in large quantities. This triggers a high state of alertness. Imagine waiting a year for a movie you've been excited to see. When that movie comes out, you sit down in the theater and are intensely focused and eager for it to start. Your brain is releasing large amounts of epinephrine and dopamine. The second neurochemical, acetylcholine, is then released from the brain. This amplifies your focus on the task at hand, or in this case the movie, such that any other sensory input you may experience becomes muted. In keeping with the analogy, you are so focused on the movie that you don't hear your partner ask you if you want more popcorn. Now, without getting even more technical, acetylcholine needs to be released from two parts of the brain in order to change it. What's important to remember is that acetylcholine acts as an amplifier to the epinephrine, such that you are alert (epinephrine) and your attention to your goal is amplified (acetylcholine.)

The third piece of the biological puzzle is this little thing called energy. Remember, our brain's primary source of energy is glucose. Alertness without energy can fade quickly. And attention without energy is short-lived. This is not an endorsement for eating large amounts of sugar before reading a book. It's simply recognizing that if we are in a depleted energy state, alertness and attention will be fleeting.

The final piece of the learning equation is perhaps the most difficult. Recall that by about the age of twenty-five, we have just about all the neurons we will ever have. Those neurons fall into two categories, the ones whose connections are strengthened through our repeated behaviors and those that are weakened by our lack of behaviors. The superhighways of our nervous system are fairly established. Which means, to learn something new, you need to re-purpose one of those established expressways. To do that, in addition to deciding what you want to learn or change, you need to decide what you will no longer do. Or, rather, what you're going to give up. As adults, we cannot learn something without first deciding on some action or behavior that we plan to not do in order to make room for the new behavior. In our experience of change, this is the step we often leave out. We rush to envision the new future version of ourselves and leave out the realization that we can only have that future self by making space. Our brains can and will adapt. But it comes at a price.

CREATING FOCUS FOR CHANGE

So, why does all this matter? It matters because we largely do not structure our learning experiences in ways that align with the chemistry of neuroplasticity. Let's take each element one by one to illustrate this.

Decision to Learn: While we often have the best of intentions when it comes to learning, we often express those goals in broad, non-specific terms. Learning requires that we attend, in the moment, to the active decision of deciding that something is worth paying attention to. We must shift from "I want to learn piano," to "I want to learn piano, now." We also often express multiple goals that compete with our attention. Focus, by definition, requires a narrow definition of what we want to achieve within a given timeframe.

Alertness: This seems circular, but focus requires alertness, and alertness requires focus. In order to learn something new, we must release epinephrine in sufficient quantities to generate mild stress, which triggers our body to focus on the task at hand. In the context of many learning experiences, there is insufficient preparation at the beginning of the learning session to trigger alertness. Either that, or rely on highly stressful, intensely emotional experiences to trigger epinephrine release. Unfortunately, these can be negative learning experiences that reinforce unproductive neural pathways.

Energy: We often contend with a range of fatigue-inducing experiences that limit our ability to learn. Sufficient sleep, exercise, diet, social connection, etc. are all elements that contribute to our physical and mental readiness to learn.

Attention: If alertness is required to generate focus, attention is required to sustain it. We are simply competing with too many sensory experiences and inputs to maintain sufficient attention on learning experiences. In addition, when we set out our numerous well-intentioned goals, we often switch between them too frequently to sustain attention.

Trade-Off: This is the death-knell of learning. Just like we must decide to learn, we must decide what to give up. In most cases, our learning objectives are a never-ending list of more. We rarely consciously decide what to give up in exchange. As a result, we can get extremely frustrated by the combined stress of learning the new behavior and frustration of not engaging in the old. Making space for learning requires that we not only focus on the present but also that we think broadly about intentional trade-offs we make in pursuit of change.

Let's put these dimensions into perspective using a real-world example. Remember my experience from 2017 when implementing the new technology system? That learning experience hits just about every single trap outlined above. First, while there was a corporate decision that employees needed to learn the new technology, it was clear that each individual in that training was on a different page. For many in that three-hour training, there were other, more important topics. Second, there was virtually no consistent alertness directed toward the learning at hand. Many people came in late for the session. The reasons the new technology was important were expressed in terms that clearly did not trigger the release of epinephrine. Or, if there was an epinephrine release, it was due to all the things the trainees could not do because they were stuck in some boring training. Third, a three-hour training, even with a break, simply extends too far beyond most people's energy reserves. Sure, there were snacks. But each person in that room was contending with whatever life circumstances that existed outside of the room. We had no idea who had eight hours of sleep instead of two, who had breakfast and who hadn't, and so on. Fourth, attention broke within minutes. Whether it was a critical phone call, email, client proposal, or something else, attention was given to the more important (as defined by the trainee) items. Without alertness and attention, we were guaranteed that little learning would occur. Finally, and most importantly, this training was just "one more thing" for the trainees to learn. In the midst of their busy jobs filled with a million things, this was one more thing for which no space, no freed-up neural pathway, was available. I recall hearing many people say things such as, "I'll just have my assistant do it," or "I'd rather keep my old spreadsheet. That is easier for me to use." No trade was being made. No choice to give something up in order for the new learning to take hold.

So how do we correct this? First, and foremost, I can't emphasize enough how important sleep is. It is the foundation of our performance and ability to change. All-nighters simply don't work for learning. Second, we know that mental focus follows visual focus. In learning sessions, begin by picking a single, narrow point in the room, on the page, etc. and train your visual focus for 60-120 seconds. Third, we can trigger the release of mild levels of adrenaline with simple breathwork. A simple sixty-second cold shower is also incredibly effective when that option is available. Finally, in addition to deciding what you'll focus on, decide what you'll give up. This might look like deciding not to pick up your phone for the sixty-minute learning session. More broadly, it might look like going to bed an hour earlier each night. Either way, that decision needs to be made. And it needs to be *your* decision.

CHAPTER 6

Strategy Five—
Generate Repetitions

"We are what we repeatedly do."
ARISTOTLE

N EARLY 2023, I STEPPED FOOT on the grounds of a nuclear power station for the first time in my life. I've worked with many different kinds of companies during my career. This was a first, for sure.

A month prior, I agreed to help the leadership team at the power station to devise a strategy to turn performance around. For the last several years, the station had slowly deteriorated. Once a shining beacon among the approximately 100 nuclear power stations in the US, the station now ranked among the bottom. Years of operational initiatives failed to show results. A year before, a new Site Vice President (the equivalent of the station CEO) had arrived at the station with the mission to change the trajectory of the station. It was a bit of a last-ditch effort to turn things around.

The station is located in a relatively rural area without many other similar employment opportunities available. As a result, generations of families have worked during the thirty-year history of the station. While this created a family-oriented culture, it also resulted in a bit of organizational stagnation.

Whether performance was high or low the employment opportunity remained. Over time, performance incrementally, almost imperceptibly, declined. As performance declined, new procedures were put in place to review performance. More checklists. More reviews. More oversight. At each turn, the response to reduced performance was to provide more oversight and reporting on the workforce to monitor performance. This, in hindsight, only made the problem worse.

The decline had reached its apex just a year before, when the station missed its planned refueling duration (a process where they change the spent nuclear fuel) by nearly double the expected time (eighty-nine days versus the planned forty-five). In the world of nuclear power, this equates to millions of dollars a day in cost and lost revenue.

A group of forty up-and-coming leaders was selected to partake in a pilot to apply the very principles we are exploring in this book.

To kick off the effort, we brought the team together for an introduction to behavior change. I had reviewed a handful of documents prior to the session. One, the employee handbook, was considered the bible for performance. It had every possible action detailed, particularly those involving safety. As one might expect, safety is the top priority at a nuclear power station. Rightly so. However, every strength is a weakness given the right circumstances. Within the handbook was a phrase that caught my eye: "When faced with uncertainty, we stop."

I built a special slide in the presentation just for this phrase. While talking about change, I flashed the slide. As I did, a voice came from the audience. "We can't change that."

"Why not?' I replied.

What transpired was a fascinating discussion that included phrases like, "We can't", "We have to", "Because", "That's required", and so on. As the team discussed, my response to that was the following. "I'm not asking you to make decisions that compromise safety. What I'm asking is where has this idea of stopping in the face of uncertainty been applied in places that have nothing to do with safety? And how is that holding you back?" Then I referenced the quote from Aristotle at the start of this chapter and reminded them that what they have created, through repetition, is a culture that stops. A culture that doesn't take initiative. A culture where people must be told what to do. And a culture that has traded the upside of performance for the comfort of low risk. They had become an organization that stops. Everywhere. Every time. No matter the circumstances.

In addition to being a prime example of repeating a behavior until it becomes engrained, the other, and perhaps more problematic behavior, was generalizing failure. In Amy Edmondson's 2023 book, *The Right Kind of Wrong,* she points out that failure is context specific and that mistakes are not the same as failures. Not all failures are equal. Of course, failures that lead to physical safety concerns at a nuclear plant are catastrophic. But there are many other instances that don't involve physical safety, where failures or mistakes may be less concerning. A failure is not the same as a mistake. Again, context and situation matter.

In the case of my client, the fear of failure had extended well beyond the physical safety dimension into many other elements of the plant to such a degree that the individual worker was unable to take action. This led to supervisors being overburdened, which slowed down work execution, which further eroded performance. In effect, in the desire to do things right, they ended up doing few things well.

To change this engrained behavior, we needed to lean into the Three Fs of learning: Frequency, Failure, and Feedback. One, we needed to frequently act independently during times of uncertainty. Two, we needed to make errors (safely). And three, we needed to get feedback while making those errors so members of the team could learn. We understood the impact of "stopping when faced with uncertainty." We needed to generate repetitions. We needed to practice failing.

A LITTLE MORE LEARNING SCIENCE

In Chapter 5, we discussed the basis for how our nervous system changes, as well as the strategies required to learn something new.

Recall that among the biggest elements of learning require that we 1) decide something is important enough to learn and 2) that we understand we must trade-off neural space to do so. That's because, after the age of twenty-five, we stop producing new neurons. From birth to roughly twenty-five, neurogenesis, or the creation of new neurons, is a feature of our nervous system. After that time, we learn through one of two mechanisms—long-term potentiation or long-term depression. Long-term potentiation (LTP) is a persistent strengthening of neural connections based on repeated patterns of activity. Long-term depression (LTD) is, quite simply, the opposite—the long-lasting decrease of neural connection strength based on a lack of use. It's the under-used space in our nervous system. When we "give up" a behavior, this is what happens within our nervous system.

The next bit of neuroscience involves what are called Central Pattern Generators (CPG). CPGs are neuronal circuits that produce rhythmic motor patterns that persist in the absence of sensory feedback or descending inputs. Recall that our autonomic nervous system controls the basic survival functions of our bodies, such as respiration, digestion, and our heartbeat. To do this, CPGs send commands to what are called lower motor neurons, which send signals to our muscles to execute those autonomic functions. We also have what are called upper motor neurons, which are involved when we engage in activities and behaviors from our somatic nervous system. When I "decide" to do something, I use the CPGs connected to my upper motor neurons to execute that deliberate action.

It was traditionally thought that CPGs sent signals to motor neurons in a one-way fashion. Signals from the brain travel down through the spine to the motor neurons to execute the movement. This is true for lower motor neurons for actions that we cannot regulate. But a growing body of evidence suggests that upper motor neurons have a feedback-inducing effect on CPGs in a two-way relationship. We can stimulate new CPGs by taking conscious actions in new ways. We can disrupt our established patterns.

Why does this matter in the world of change and transformation? Well, because every person, including you, arrives at a change experience with different sets of behaviors we repeat and avoid, and therefore a unique set of established patterns of behaviors (CPGs). If we are to shift these patterns, we need to act in ways that open up neuroplasticity. Which is to say we need to disrupt those patterns to trigger an awareness that our established routines and approaches are ineffective. In short, we need to make errors.

THE IMPORTANCE OF ERRORS

Acknowledging Amy Edmondson's reasoned and important distinction between failures and mistakes, we'll use a different word: errors. Understanding that context and magnitude have a significant role to play in our assessment of what is a mistake and what is an error for the purposes of our understanding of change, we'll use the word "error" to signal any action or deviation that is out of sync with our expectations or objectives.

It turns out that when we make an error, our brain is immediately signaled that something needs to be fixed. As you'll recall from Chapter 5, when our brain is intensely focused on a particular item, it opens the possibility for plasticity by triggering the release of epinephrine (alertness) and acetylcholine (attention). Errors, particularly errors of our own creation, rapidly accelerate this process. The more errors you make, the more plastic your brain becomes.

The challenge, of course, is that most people don't respond well to the experience of making errors. For all sorts of reasons, we strive to succeed, both in our eyes and in the eyes of others. Look no further than my client, who encouraged stopping when faced with uncertainty. This policy was nothing more than a procedural incentive to not make mistakes. To get it right. Walking away from the possibilities of making errors creates long-term depression in our neural pathways for risk, while creating long-term potentiation for safer behavior. The result is that an error, any error, is discouraged. This, in turn, reduces the ability to learn.

Walking away from errors is the wrong behavior for learning. Anything.

If we can stay with the process of making errors (within appropriate safety boundaries), we'll create a central pattern generator (CPG) for learning itself. To do so, recall in Chapter 4 we discussed changing our relationship with stress. If we can work through an experience, particularly our emotional experience of stress, we'll recruit enough dopamine to complement epinephrine and acetylcholine and learn rapidly. Also, recall that when we engage in actions that are deliberately difficult, we increase the size of our Anterior Mid-Cingulate Cortex (aMCC), the air-traffic control center of our brains. Finally, recall that our brains are prediction machines. To help with the complexity, let me say it simply—we change when we can withstand the discomfort of making errors when attempting to learn new behaviors. People who can tolerate and push through the experience of failure do well in life. For themselves, for their teams, and for their organizations.

Tolerating errors, however, is easier said than done. As children, we can rapidly adjust both our physical movement and behavioral patterns. Large errors tend to have a less negative impact on our ability to try again. The flexibility of one's young nervous system allows for rapid assignment and re-assignment of behaviors. Our central pattern generators aren't too fixed yet. When combined with the fact that we are building new neurons, withstanding failure becomes a pretty organic feature. We can even adjust our nervous system to inaccurate environmental cues, as demonstrated by Eric Knudsen, Stanford neuroscientist, and his famous experiments involving the visual and auditory fields of barn owls. As adults, however, the story changes.

Knudsen and his colleagues demonstrated that conditions that lead to near-complete auditory map adjustment in juvenile owls induce little plasticity in adult owls. The adult brain just doesn't handle rapid plasticity the way it does when we are young. Except, interestingly, when we are pursuing food.

In those same studies, it was demonstrated that when we are hungry focused on basic survival, our brain responds with the same epinephrine, acetylcholine, and dopamine combinations of a much younger brain. Why? Because I can't imagine anything we need to pay attention to more than the pursuit of the very thing that keeps us alive: food. The adult nervous system can tolerate errors; they must just be smaller and occur more frequently. Given what we now know about learning, which requires the strengthening of existing neural pathways, the primary route to changing one's brain comes from repeating a new, desired action. We need to generate repetitions.

GENERATING REPETITIONS

In his famous book *Outliers: The Story of Success*, Malcolm Gladwell discussed the 10,000 rule—the idea that it takes 10,000 hours to become an expert within a given field. While there's been some debate about the validity of this measure (and the purpose of this book is not to prove or disprove the specific rule), what Gladwell got right in his assessment of what builds skill is repetition. The precise amount will vary greatly from person-to-person and skill-to-skill. Lots of repetition. And it's not just any repetition. It's highly focused, specialized, learning-based repetition that matters.

In 2019, Mark Rober gave a TED Talk that has now been viewed over forty million times. In this now famous talk, Mark detailed what he called "The Super Mario Effect."

Mark and his colleagues ran a brief experiment where they demonstrated the impact that errors, and the perception of loss associated with those errors, on our willingness to persist. It turns out, from his fun little online coding experiment, that when people lose something of value (in this case, five fictitious internet points) when they make a mistake, they are less likely to try again. However, when we simply receive feedback that we have made a mistake, with no corollary negative impact, we try again. When there is no "loss" associated with the error, we try at a rate of almost two-times higher than if we lose. Remember my client's policy of "when faced with uncertainty, we stop." There was a risk of loss associated with action. So, people stopped trying. They stopped generating repetitions. If you're curious, just search "Mark Rober, The Super Mario Effect" and you'll learn why he calls it that.

We now understand that the neurobiological basis for learning is to perform as many repetitions and errors as you possibly can within a given learning session. So how do we do that? Well, let's recall the beginning of this chapter where I talked about our understanding of motor neuron learning. First, as discussed in Chapter 5, we must identify the one element we want to change. And here our eyes can't be bigger than our stomachs. It must be *one*. Lest we forget the Quitters Day phenomenon of stacking too many resolutions on each other. Second, we must structure our learning sessions in ninety-minute cycles. These respond to our natural ultradian rhythms.

First identified by Nathaniel Kleitman, considered the godfather of modern sleep science, ultradian rhythms are alternating periods of high-frequency brain activity (about ninety minutes) followed by lower-frequency brain activity (about twenty minutes). Then, according to Dr. Andrew Huberman, you should structure the ninety-minute period as follows:

- Ten to fifteen minutes to focus on the task at hand. Leverage visual focus (Chapter 5) to trigger alertness and attention.

- Generate as many repetitions as you can within the next twenty to thirty minutes, with a particular emphasis on making errors. This can include errors in information recall, in a particular movement pattern, etc.

- Put the material down and take a five-minute pause.

- Spend the next ten minutes or so working back through the material to identify the point where you couldn't recall the information. Identify that point.

Next, do nothing. That's right. Get up. Walk away from the material. Take a walk. Close your eyes for ten minutes. Sit quietly. But you need to pause and let your brain record the material you've just covered. The term that Dr. Huberman uses to describe this experience is Non-Sleep Deep Rest (NSDR). And it's a critical element of the learning experience.

This is one of the big mistakes we all make in learning and why the modern-day schedule is so detrimental to learning. The deluge of meetings and activities, when combined with the sheer diversity of tasks that we must accomplish, make it difficult to learn. More importantly, there's rarely much transition time between those activities. No rest period.

It is important to acknowledge that learning is possible outside of this general structure. So-called one-trial learning is possible when an experience is emotionally salient, particularly negative emotional experiences. This is also true if something surprises us. We tend to trigger neuroplasticity. These one-trial experiences, while potentially formative, are generally not to be relied upon for sustained, long-term potentiation.

Critical to the learning experience is the idea of associating errors with progress. Recall in Chapter 3 we discussed how we can restructure our goals in a fashion that creates increased motivation. We are more motivated when we begin a new activity and when we get close to finishing. If we can associate errors with progress toward the path to learning, we can recruit more dopamine to sustain our performance. Remember that simply the subjective belief that something is good for us is sufficient for creating increased dopamine. More errors, more progress. More progress, more dopamine. More dopamine, more repetitions. More repetitions, more influence on our upper motor neurons and our central pattern generator for learning.

ERRORS AND FEEDBACK

One of my favorite books is *The Inner Game of Tennis* by Timothy Gallwey. If you haven't read it, I suggest you do. In the event you want to read it, I'll try not to over summarize the key concepts.

During his time as a tennis coach, Gallwey realized that in the well-intentioned spirit of coaching his players, he was, in fact, over coaching them. Fix this. Do that. Stand here. Swing there. The more he brought their awareness to a particular point of correction, the more they focused on the needed correction . . . often to their detriment. What Gallwey realized was the less he said, the better the athlete performed. More importantly, instead of pointing out the need for corrections, he simply coached them to bring their awareness to an action, without prescribing the necessary remedy. Like The Super Mario Effect experiment, the best feedback was simply to identify the action was wrong and for the players to try again.

Recall that when we can create focus on the learning experience and especially when we create errors, we open the gateway to neuroplasticity. It is our ability to self-diagnose errors that is most impactful. In addition, as we progress in our abilities, we are able to more acutely direct our attention to specific movements. For example, my son plays quarterback at our local high school. I've coached him since he was seven years old. At age seven, my role was to provide basic instruction on throwing mechanics and techniques. Over the years, he required less instruction on specific mechanics because he was able to self-identify when he made a physical error. As he progressed, my role shifted to more nuanced coaching around game strategy. Once he got better at identifying his own physical mistakes, he got better at correcting them. Then he learned more about game strategy and was able to cue his attention to the mental side of the game while his central pattern generators for throwing mechanics operated without him even having to think about them. On the rare occasion that he misses a throw, I simply need to ask him, "What happened there?" and he's able to tell me in detail what error occurred on the throw. Had I told him his error, his brain would not be as plastic as it is when he is able to perceive and evaluate the error.

This speaks to the nature of feedback, as well as to the role of coaches. Without over-analyzing the definition and role of a coach, we can all agree that a coach is someone who imparts knowledge and feedback to a person or a group of people to improve their knowledge or skill. Coaches do this by providing instruction, observation, and feedback. In the pursuit of change and transformation, understanding what we now know about how we learn as adults, a coach should do three things. First, help you create the conditions for learning success. Second, provide a foundation of knowledge for which you can generate repetitions and failures. Third, and most importantly, help you sustain focus and effort through errors. It is not to correct the errors. That is your responsibility.

You might be thinking, "How do I generate repetitions for behavior?" The answer can be found in an approach introduced in Chapter 3— breaking down our behaviors into component pieces.

Let's take the example of a difficult conversation with a co-worker. While it is certainly not serving a tennis ball, which requires foot placement, back extension, racket position, eye focus, follow through, and so on, it contains a bevy of specific, distinct responses and reactions around which we can narrow our attention:

Listening: Am I fully engaged in listening to understand and withholding judgement from what I'm hearing?

Questioning: Am I asking questions that support greater understanding of my co-workers' points and emotions?

Breathing: Am I breathing effectively to help regulate any emotional frustration I may be experiencing?

Speaking: Am I maintaining a non-combative, even tone in my voice?

Connecting: Am I maintaining eye contact and a positive physical position to invite conversation?

Responding: Am I responding with thoughtful responses instead of reacting emotionally?

Each of these actions originates from a central pattern generator over which we have an ability to influence and modify. We have upper motor neurons that take instruction from our brain, in many cases with little thought, because we are transacting through a discussion. But, if we can bring our attention to each of these behavioral elements, if we focus, then we are able to create new, intentional repetitions to shift our behavior. In each experience, we can make errors and with each error we can make an intentional adjustment.

Finding ways to practice desired changes, and making errors while doing so, is a cornerstone of change. We must do this far more frequently than we likely desire. When we do it with a coach who can help us turn our attention toward key behavior patterns, we increase our chances of success. And as we increasingly get better at our new behavior, we can direct our own awareness to greater and greater levels of sophistication. As we progress, it will be time to focus on another behavior. And time to make new errors. Rinse and repeat.

There's no question that learning new behaviors as adults is challenging. Our brains simply don't learn the same way as when we were younger. It is often the experience of learning and the frustration of making errors that prevent us from pushing through. Errors are a signal to us, not to stop, but to keep going. When we train our focus on the benefits of errors, we prepare our brains for the very changes we seek. When we combine this reflection with feedback from coaches, we increase our chance of transformation success. Feedback, internal or external, is the signal needed to correct our errors. When we can embrace this iterative experience of frequency, failure, and feedback, we build a literal central pattern generator for growth itself. Then it's just a matter of pointing that CPG at the next opportunity to change.

CHAPTER 7

Strategy Six— Reward Progress

"It's not the destination, it's the journey."
RALPH WALDO EMERSON

WE HAVE ARRIVED AT the sixth and final strategy, Reward Progress.

Here's a short description of what we've learned:

- **Shift Environment**: We can shift our four primary environments to create constraints and access to behavior change.

- **Initiate Movement**: We can influence our dopamine and goal definition to create the motivation and movement we need to achieve our goals.

- **Embrace Stress**: Short-term stress is required for growth, and we must rebuild our relationship with stress to fuel change.

- **Create Focus**: Changing our nervous system requires alertness and attention, as well as the conscious decision to make room for new learning.

- **Generate Repetitions**: We learn through strengthening existing neural pathways and/or weakening others, which requires that we repeat intentional actions and make errors to correct.

I've placed Reward Progress as the last of the six strategies because, in many ways, how we measure our path to and through change is one of the biggest reasons we give up. Remember Quitters Day, Jan 19? That's the day that most people give up on their New Year's resolutions. Why? Because three weeks into their goal pursuit, the change feels either too hard, too slow, or too ineffective. We stop, not because we aren't making progress. We stop because we don't see progress soon enough. And we become discouraged.

What Chapter 6 taught is that change takes repetition. A lot of repetition. Over a long period of time.

All the strategies we've learned provide us with the foundation to understand how to leverage our brains, bodies, and biology to create change. But it is often the *time* it takes to change that stands in our way. As I often remind my clients, progress is directional, not absolute. When we reframe our understanding of the rewards of change, we are better positioned to maintain the effort and focus required to do so.

To illustrate this, let me take you back to the team of people I introduced you to in Chapter 6. When we started the behavior-shift program, the station was one year away from their next refueling outage. Recall that in their last refueling outage, they nearly doubled the intended time. Refueling outages are a bit like the Super Bowl in this world. And at their last Super Bowl, they didn't just lose. They got stomped. The goal of the behavior-shift program was to correct this. They didn't just need to win. They needed to win BIG! The challenge was threefold. One, if the best predictor of future performance was past performance, they weren't exactly building off positive momentum. Two, and more importantly, the goal was a year away. How were they going to change their behavior now for something they couldn't prove would work for another year? Three, we had the added challenge of needing to change close to 800 people.

As we learned in Chapter 3, dopamine tends to be highest when we are starting something, as well as nearing the finish line. But, like Quitters Day, it is that messy middle experience that often meets with the biggest resistance. We were able to keep momentum high during the three months of the pilot program, although each week I had to answer the question "How do we do this [behavior shift] and our regular job?" This, of course, requires that people understand that this is their job. And it is this question that perfectly encapsulates a critical piece of change—the more we consider the pursuit of change as separate and apart from who we are as individuals or what we do daily, the more friction we create in achieving it. The more I focus on how much weight I lost today, for example, the harder it is to maintain focus on losing weight because my single-day results are very small when compared to the big, audacious goal I set. In short, the farther away the goal, the harder it is to sustain my momentum.

To fix this problem, we identified five behavior shifts which would positively impact overall station performance. Not just for the outage, but everywhere. This operates on the principle that "the way we do some things is the way we do everything." Each of the forty members picked one shift, sometimes two, that would be their primary focus (Create Focus) for the next three months. At the end of three months, they would focus on another primary shift and would continue this leading up to their outage. By the time the outage arrived, each participant would have had sufficient time to build (e.g., Generate Repetitions) most of the new behaviors. The goal was not to focus on the outage a year from now, but on practicing the new behaviors. For each individual, they turned their focus away from a year from now to the actions they could generate today. Practicing new behaviors became the goal.

Wondering if it worked? In March of 2024, the station met the twenty-eight-day target exactly. To put their performance in perspective, it was the first sub-thirty-day outage since 2007 and the best outage in the company since 2012.

Let's talk about why this approach worked.

NOUNS AND TIME

One of our biggest change mistakes is that we define our goals in nouns. We visualize the future and imagine the objects of attainment (new house, new car, new job) or states of being (happier, thinner, richer) that we desire. These are things. Inherently, there is nothing wrong with these things. But there are dangers in defining our goals as things (nouns). The first, as we discussed a moment ago, is that they tend to be far away in time. We know through countless studies that we value benefits which are far off into the future far less than benefits we can have today. Second, goals defined as nouns tend to be binary. We either achieve them or we don't. Or at least that's how we imagine it. Third, they are often attached to our happiness / satisfaction. The "I'll be happy when . . ." experience. This creates a bit of a perfect storm. A goal that's far away, for which we either reach it or we don't, and we won't be happy until we do. Welcome to the roots of Quitters Day.

Recall in Chapter 1 that our brains are predictions machines. It also turns out that our brains are time machines as well. Based on the work of UCLA neuroscientist Dean Buonomano, we humans possess the unique ability to understand the past, present, and future. While this may seem uninteresting to each of us, it is what makes us uniquely human. It is critical for how we estimate, and communicate, our goals . . . as well as our progress toward those goals.

Let's look at our three forms of time perception a little more clinically. The easy one is present time. This is our perception of how quickly, or not, things happen in real time. There is prospective time, which is how we envision time transpiring going forward. Think of it as how long a week's worth of time into the future may seem for you. And there is retrospective time, or how we remember time in the past. The alignment of these perceptions and experiences is something science calls entrainment.

It turns out that our biology, specifically our hormones, plays a large role in entrainment and how we perceive each of these time dimensions. Dopamine, and its close cousin epinephrine, have the effect of increasing our perception of time. The more dopamine and/or epinephrine that are released, the more we increase our frame rate and slice time into more granular increments. When dopamine is high, a minute might feel like ten or fifteen. This is true for something that is both highly stressful and something we consider very fun. For this reason, a two-minute cold shower feels like a lifetime and that family trip to Disneyland seems to go by in a flash. Serotonin, on the other hand, has the opposite effect. The more serotonin released, the more that time seems to drag on. Under a heavy influence of serotonin, five minutes might feel like an hour. Just ask my son when I make him meditate for five minutes.

The effects of dopamine and serotonin on retrospective time shift a bit. Consider the two-minute cold shower example. Under the stress of the cold, dopamine increases, and time slows. We experience each fine grain element of that experience in ways that make it feel much longer than two minutes. However, when it's over, we tend to view that experience as less painful than it was. This is the result of increased serotonin. Similarly, when we experience something that is fun, that time goes by in a flash. We tend to look back on the experience and remember each tiny element in more detail. The effects of dopamine on prospective time can be just as tricky and result in us believing that the goal is closer than it is. Or, more accurately, that we believe we can accomplish it faster than is actually possible. With a higher frame rate of excitement and expectation, we are likely to overestimate our abilities, as well as the proximity to our goal. We think it's closer than it is. Meanwhile, under heavy serotonin influence, when we are doing something we believe is mundane or boring, it feels like it will take forever to get to our goals. I often call this the "college graduation experience." When we arrive at college, the prospect of our graduation seems daunting and, quite literally, years away. Each year, semester, class, project, etc. is filled with experiences and activities that seem complex and difficult. These feel as if they drag on. In between these difficult moments and experiences are moments of exhilaration and joy, which go by in a flash. And then, on the day of our graduation we look back and say two things: "that went by fast" and "that wasn't so bad."

How does this relate to how we measure progress? Well, when we are off in our expectations of how long we think something should take versus how long it actually takes, we create entrainment gaps. This leads to quitting. But, if we understand how to use time perception in the other direction, we can create greater alignment of our perception and our experience of the time it takes to change. To do that, let's look a little deeper at the brain's reward system.

THE BRAIN'S REWARD CIRCUITRY

The brain's reward circuity is the part of the brain that tells us something about our environment is reinforcing and/or rewarding. In this case, reinforcing is defined as a behavior that leads to a particular stimulus that you enjoy, something you want to do again. Rewarding is simply an enjoyable experience. This distinction is important because these experiences are not equivalent. In short, we can exhibit behaviors that are reinforcing, but not rewarding. The most extreme instance of this is found in the world of addiction. We all can think of numerous examples of things that we want to do, but we understand those things are either not good for us or not always the experience we believe they would be. What's important to understand is that this can work in reverse as well. There are experiences that are not rewarding (at least as defined in the present moment of our salient experience) but are reinforcing. Perhaps, for example, having a particularly difficult workout or a tough conversation with a co-worker. A hard workout might not feel good while you're experiencing them, but we understand potential long-term benefits.

The purpose of our brain's reward circuitry is straightforward. We need a signal that allows us to move toward desirable actions that promote our survival and steer us away from actions that endanger it. At its most basic level, we find this in reproduction and in survival from predators. As a social species, we guaranteed our survival by being close to potential mates and by leveraging the protection of the group. Of course, most of us don't face these kinds of immediate dangers in today's world, although mating remains a social behavior where we require interaction with others.

While these are the two most basic instances of reward circuitry, the patterns apply to everything we do. What we have come to understand is that when dopamine is activated, we become attached to that experience. And, according to Dr. Robert Malenka, Pritzker Professor of Psychiatry and Behavioral Sciences at Stanford, "while we understand that dopamine is the trigger, the truth is that we still don't understand the deep mechanics of why dopamine is so rewarding. We just know it is." But what can glean both from scientific literature and from our understanding of dopamine is the following: If the brain's reward circuitry is heavily tied to the experience of (primarily) dopamine, and dopamine is most active while we are in the pursuit of our desires, then the brain's reward circuitry is most active while in pursuit. It is about striving and reaching for those behaviors that are reinforcing and/ rewarding. Or avoiding experiences that are not rewarding or those that are painful. In short, it's either about moving towards, or away.

REDEFINING SUCCESS

And here lies the paradox. We envision our goals as objects or states of being in the *future*. A future where our perception of the time required to achieve it is not aligned with actual time. When we imagine our future self, we experience the neurochemical hit of dopamine from imagining our success. The image of the goal is rewarding. And yet, the behavior to attain it does not feel reinforcing. It requires effort. It's difficult. It's stressful. We want to reach the goal, but we don't like the stress of going to get it. And yet, what our brain needs is pursuit. It needs a struggle. After all, stress is required for change. But because we don't always experience the stress as rewarding, we stop. And we know that when the brain stops striving, motivation erodes. And the goal never appears.

How can we reconcile this paradox? We must change the definition of success. We must reward the effort exerted in pursuit of the goal. *Not the goal itself.* We must measure the actions (verbs) that lead up to our goals (nouns). Effort must become the reward. As with Amy Edmondson's assertion that failure is context specific, it turns out that rewards are also context specific. We can assign a reward to anything. Rewards are subjective. How can we do that? The answer lies no farther than the "stress-is-enhancing" mindset we explored in Chapter 4.

Here's a little story to demonstrate this. My sixteen-year-old son is an exceptional baseball player. And in the case of a sport like baseball, exceptional means you fail just a bit less than other players. Remember, as a hitter, if you're successful just thirty percent of the time, you're considered one of the best. If only one in three plate appearances results in the player getting a hit, how can you redefine success so you don't get so discouraged from failure that you quit the sport altogether? The answer: redefine a successful at bat.

When my son was twelve, his baseball coach gave him a way to think about hitting that forever changed his view of success, but at the same time managed to give him the secret to rewarding progress. My son was in the midst of a strong season and on more than one occasion, he was the recipient of a "lucky" hit. For example, he might put the ball in play, and it got a funky bounce away from the infielder. Once the ball literally hit a small imperfection on the field and jumped six feet in the air over the infielder. But then, things started to turn, and those lucky bounces started turning into outs. My son became increasingly frustrated because the outcome was turning away from his favor. But ironically, he hadn't been doing anything differently. He had defined success as the noun of "being safe at first" irrespective of the actions he took.

So, one day after what he considered an unsuccessful day, his coach pulled him aside and told him that being successful at bat includes three things. First, asking, "Did I swing at the pitch I was looking for?" Second, "Did I swing with my good swing?" Meaning, "Was my form and technique the best it could be?" And third, "IF there was contact, did I give maximum effort in running to first base?" This, quite simply, is gold. Let's look at each piece.

First, "Did I get the pitch I was looking for?" Was he intently focused on the pitch that was most important to him? Remember our discussion from Chapter 5, Create Focus? Second was the question, "Did I swing my good swing?" When the opportunity arose to act, the question the coach wanted him to ask himself was, "Did I act with my best attempt?" Note that it is about the quality of his swing, which is what he controlled. And the final question the coach suggested he ask himself was, "Did I give maximum effort running to first base?" Again, effort. Did he push as hard as possible? Nowhere in the definition of a successful at-bat is arriving safely at first base. Success is about the effort and input the hitter controls. Not on the outcome.

This is how we must redefine and reward change success. Success, and progress toward change, comes on the attempt, on the effort involved in progressing towards one's goals.

This doesn't just apply in the world of baseball. In a famous 1998 study, again by Carol Dweck, research found that praising children for their intelligence reduces their motivation and performance. Instead, when we praise children for their effort, not only do they generally perform better on tasks, but they also tend to pick tasks and activities that are more difficult. Praising children for effort results in them willingly choosing to do progressively hard things. It prompts them to change. Instead of focusing on performance outcomes, they focus on the effort and process of learning. They focus on having a good at-bat, not getting on base.

Focusing on effort has the added benefit of offsetting the challenges with our perception of time as well. When effort towards change is the reward, we focus less on how far away the goal is and return our focus, and dopamine release, to the present moment. This reinforces our sense of how much effort we give and, by extension, how much we accomplish in each attempt. This is exactly what each individual at the nuclear power station did. Each person focused on building the behaviors that led to learning and change. They focused on the attempts and effort of change by defining a set of behaviors that constitute having a good "at-bat." Then they focused on getting as many quality at-bats as they could. They focused on executing the repetitions of change. And when their colleagues worked hard at attempting to change, they praised each other for the effort. They especially praised each other when one made an error and kept going. It's akin to one of your teammates striking out their last time up and continuing to encourage them to have a great at-bat the next time they are up. This is how we change.

If you needed more evidence of how this works, look back to an exceptional TED Talk from Adam Grant in 2016 called *The Surprising*

Habits of Original Thinkers. In this talk Adam says, "If you look across fields, the greatest originals are the ones who fail the most. Because they are the ones who try the most." His evidence? Just a few people named Thomas Edison, Johan Bach, and Mozart. When you look at the volume of work they produced in their lifetime, it was the sheer number of attempts at greatness that distinguishes them from their peers. They simply took more swings than others.

TEAM EFFORT

Throughout this book, I've referred to the highly social nature of the human species. I've also referenced the idea that social behaviors are among the most biologically rewarding behaviors we can engage in. While this seems obvious, thanks to the work of Dr. Kay Tye, Professor of Systems Neurobiology at the Salk Institute for Biological Studies and a Howard Hughes Medical Institute (HHMI) Investigator, we understand more about the biology of social interactions than ever before. This all starts with the amygdala.

Most of the narrative around the amygdala centers on it being the center of the fight-or-flight system. As discussed in Chapter 4, the amygdala is the beginning of the stress chain, which determines if we should move towards or away from a stimulus. What we now know is that the amygdala plays a role in assigning positive or negative associations to all our experiences, not just the ones associated with stress. Through Dr. Tye's work we also understand the tremendous positive benefits that social interactions imbue, as well as the deleterious effects of social isolation. There has also been deep research into the social striving experiences of children and the role the positive association with group dynamics plays in our lives. Study after study shows that children go to great lengths to fit into social structures.

Why do I bring this up? The same part of the brain involved in the stress response also assigns a positive association with experiences. We understand that the most dopamine we produce is during stress and/or in the experience of striving towards our goals. And we also know that when we are close to other people, we create critical bonding hormones such as serotonin and oxytocin. What we can conclude is that when we are striving and producing effort that is directed towards others and meaningful to them, we can create a perfect storm of biological rewards for change. This is why firefighters, military servicemen and women, athletes in team sports, and others in similar environments all recount the incredible bonds they form with the men and women they have gone into danger with.

I also bring this up to highlight the experience at the nuclear power station. What made that experience particularly effective was that several members of the same group were going through the same experience at once. In moments of stress and discomfort, members of the group could lean on each other for support. In addition, the group created additional motivation, i.e., dopamine, by sharing successes and challenges with each other. Learning was expanded as feedback was shared among the group as well. All of this, and more, turned what would normally be considered a stressful experience for any one individual into an experience that their brains redefined as positive. The individual behaviors they were shifting became less important than the idea that their brains began to associate the experience of shifting behavior as positive. The effort involved in shifting became the goal.

While neuroscience mechanisms might be complex, the conclusions are straightforward. When we define the reward of change as being that of the effort involved in making a change, we improve our ability to achieve our goals. And, when we can do that with a group of people that share in the same experience, we harness the full power of our social nature to accelerate change. We are goal directed, and striving is an essential need for our brain. And we are simultaneously a social species that needs support from and contribution to others. In short, if you want to change, direct your effort towards a goal that serves others, and you'll provide your brain with an incredible source of motivation.

CHAPTER 8

Change Starts with You

*"Every block of stone has a statue inside it,
and it is the task of the sculptor to discover it."*
MICHELANGELO

O N NOVEMBER 1, 1512, Michelangelo Buonarroti introduced the world to one of the most spectacular works of art ever created—the ceiling fresco of the Sistine Chapel. Located in the heart of Vatican City, the Sistine Ceiling covers 12,000 square feet and depicts scenes from the Old Testament. Along with scenes from *The Last Judgement*, also painted by Michelangelo from 1534 to 1541, on the west wall behind the altar, these frescoes are considered the crowning achievement of Renaissance art.

People come from around the world to see the Sistine Chapel. I'm lucky enough to have seen it twice. I was two classes away from an Art History minor in college and have always had a passion for Renaissance art. As someone who has almost no artist ability, I'm in awe of the incredible mastery involved in the artwork, as well as captivated by the idea that the artwork remains central to our human experience more than 500 years after its completion. I'll be impressed if this book lasts for ten years! If you can see the Sistine Chapel in your lifetime, I can't recommend it enough. It is a timeless feat of human creation.

You might wonder what a book about change and transformation would have to do with the Sistine Chapel. The answer lies in the intersection of art and science—the title of this book. When one looks at the Sistine Ceiling, we see the vivid colors, the striking musculature of the figures, and the storytelling of the Creation laid against other scenes of the Life of Christ and the Last Judgment. This incredible artistry encapsulates the sum of Christian history in one place, beautifully constructed and visually unequaled. But there's more to the story.

Behind the astonishing beauty of the Sistine Ceiling is . . . science. To complete this stunning work of art, Michelangelo applied his knowledge of science and math to ensure that what your eye sees is perfectly constructed. First, the fresco is painted from the perspective of someone standing at the back of the chapel, opposite the main altar. Using foreshortening and atmospheric perspective, Michelangelo measured and aligned the figures in a fashion that mimicked the geometry of looking at the physical objects from that distance as if they were physically there. What's even more impressive is that this was done on a domed ceiling in a manner that gives the illusion that it's flat. You can see similar proportional design in sculptures like the David. When viewing the David straight on, one notices the elongated limbs and enlarged hands. The reason for this is that the David was originally placed high atop the roof of the Opera del Duomo cathedral in Florence. A similar technique was used to paint the Sistine Ceiling. And, in a final stroke of mathematical genius, the space in the famous central panel between the hands of Adam and God is separated by The Golden Ratio. The Golden Ratio (also known as Phi, or the Fibonacci number) is the mathematical symmetry algorithm that underlies our perception of attractiveness. This ratio is ubiquitous in nature, from flower petals, to pinecones, to the geometry of shells, to the distance ratios of celestial galaxies.

The Sistine Ceiling is one of history's most famous works of art because it is also an astonishing feat of mathematics. Why does this matter in the world of change? Because it is the intersection of science and our application of that science that results in our ability to change. Knowing the science of change is one thing. Being able to put that science into practice and designing a tapestry of change that works for you is another.

This is the art of change. We must know the foundational principles, but then we must understand the context of how, when, where, and even if we should apply them. Each of us is a canvas or a raw block of stone where our life experience has already painted or sculpted a set of patterns, images, ratios, etc. that reflect the unique map of our lived experience. Imagine Michelangelo arriving at the Sistine Chapel to find that paintings had already begun on the ceiling. In fact, work on the David had already begun by other artists and Michelangelo built off their starting point. In fact, those previous artists had stopped sculpting because there were imperfections in the grain of the stone. I find this to be a beautiful analogy of our very human experience of change.

For each of us, we arrive at the change journey an unfinished sculpture waiting to be completed. With our imperfect, unfinished casts, we approach change filled with both our past and the possibility of our future. Like Michelangelo, we must understand how to translate the science of change into a work of art. Thus far, we have explored six strategies for change rooted in scientific principles. However, while there may be a formula change, change is not formulaic. In the pages that follow, we'll explore how to build your unique formula for change. We'll look at how we start with your unfinished painting to combine those scientific principles to create your own individual masterpiece of change.

THE TRUTH ABOUT CHANGE

I'm going to let you in on a little secret. It's not something we often hear, and in the world of change, it's rarely talked about. In addition, it's a bit controversial. To quote Jack Nicholson's character, Colonel Jessup, from the movie *A Few Good Men*, "deep down in places you don't talk about at parties," there is a truth staring us in the face that we tend to set aside at best, or ignore at worst.

The only person you can change is you.

Let me say that again.

The only person you can change is you.

In the world of change and transformation, it's appealing to look to others—our family members, our teams, our companies, heck, our society—and say, "you should change." We are quick to point out the ways in which others fall short, need to think differently, and so on. But the reality we face is that we do not, and cannot, control another person. At best, we can influence them. And, from my experience, we influence best through leading by example. When it comes to helping people change, we do that by changing ourselves. By applying the six core change principles to our lives, and demonstrating through our success and our failures, we show that change is possible. When we paint our own masterpiece or chisel our own sculpture, we inspire others to do the same.

Now that we have the truth out of the way, there's one small item left to discuss. And that's why we fail at change. Or, better said, how the mistakes we make lead us not to change. Remember, errors and failure are an important part of the process. The journey to change ourselves is filled with obstacles. Many of which we don't see. Many we see and ignore. But if we are to change ourselves, we must understand what lies ahead. Applying the six science-backed strategies is not simply, as we learned from Michelangelo, a matter of knowing. To create our work of art, we must understand the trappings that lie before us. Let's lay them out one at a time.

CHANGE CHALLENGE #1
Too many changes at once

Referenced several times in this book is Quitter's Day. Quitter's Day, or January 19th, is the day that most people give up on their New Year's resolutions. Nineteen days. That's all it takes. Why? Well, the reasons are many and we discussed them previously. But one of the largest contributors is that we simply try to make too many changes at once. Eat better. Exercise more. Get more sleep. Be a better spouse. A better parent. Read more. Work less. The list goes on and on. In the world of change, our eyes are often much bigger than our stomachs. When it comes to change, less is more. Or rather, fewer is more. Fewer things on the list of things we want to change.

CHANGE CHALLENGE #2
Poor conditions for success

We spoke earlier about the importance of creating the conditions to be successful. It's not just the desire to change. It's about the system we each create to enable change. We discussed the power of our environment, the role of coaches, the importance of feedback, for example. When we embark on a change journey, we often fail to address the conditions around us that improve our chances of success. We rely on our willpower and grit alone. While willpower and grit are important attributes—resilience is essential—we must look at the architecture of our interactions, environment, relationships, and more, in order to successfully change.

CHANGE CHALLENGE #3
Waiting until we are ready.

There's no magic to January 1st. Or the 19th, for that matter. Change can happen at any time. There's an old saying that says, "The best time to plant a tree was ten years ago. The second-best time is now." Every day we wait to change is one less day we are making progress toward our goals. Chapter 3 talks about the importance of initiating movement. Waiting is the death knell of transformation.

CHANGE CHALLENGE #4
Not understanding the behavior to change.

In Chapter 7, we explored the difference between reinforcing and rewarding behavior. We often focus our change effort on rewarding behaviors, e.g., what feels good, when, instead, we should focus on our reinforcing behaviors, i.e., our triggers. These are often difficult to identify and even more difficult to modify.

CHANGE CHALLENGE #5
Giving up too early.

Change will always take longer than we wish. Quitter's Day is evidence of this. We've established that change takes time. A good rule of thumb is to focus on one change goal per quarter. There will, of course, be variance depending on the goal and your situation. But, in general, think about four change goals per year. Any more than that and we run into the potential Quitter's Day situation.

Change Challenge #6
Focus on outcomes.

Speaking of goals, as we've already discussed, when we focus only on the outcomes of our change journey, we struggle to maintain motivation and focus. Since we don't lose thirty pounds in one day, let alone ninety days, it can be deflating when we don't see our results as quickly as we'd like. As we discussed in Chapter 7, effort must become the goal.

The question that stands before us then is, given all that we know and given all that we know can go wrong with change, how do we do it? How do we put it all together?

The answer is simple. Three questions and four phases.

THREE QUESTIONS THAT CAN CHANGE YOUR LIFE

I get two questions most often about change: "What should I change?" And "How do I change?" When people ask me that, my response is generally, "Well, that depends. What in your life are you struggling with?" Notice I didn't say, "What do you want to achieve?" I asked what is causing them difficulty. I get a lot of different answers. Mostly framed as goals. Some are specific. Most tend to be general. Be better at X. Do more of Y. Do less of Z. Sometimes all of them together! But, in almost every case, whether it is at work or in their personal life, I tell my clients to ask themselves three questions. Three simple questions. When answered—and I mean REALLY answered—the results can change your life.

QUESTION #1
How have I done [something] in the past?

We all have patterns. As we learned in Chapter 5 from Dr. Merzenich, by the time we are in our mid-twenties, our brains are a customized map of our unique experience. That customized map contains the patterns we have developed through repeated actions. The thing is, many of us don't recognize that these patterns have developed. While we, of course, continue to learn, a large portion of our preferences and patterns are established by then. From extreme examples such as early life trauma to the more innocuous fact that most of us stop listening to new music after the age of twenty-seven (and eleven months, to be precise).

This question requires that we evaluate our actions, motivations, triggers, etc. When we articulate a desire to change something in our life, we must dig deep to understand and evaluate all the ways in which we behaved up to this point. If our goal is to lose weight, how have we tried to maintain a fitness program previously? You want to ask yourself questions such as "Why did I start? Why did I stop? What did I enjoy? What did I hate? What are the stories I told myself along the way?" Really digging into the reflection of how our past selves have contributed to our current selves is the basis for how we start to identify what needs to change. It's important that we don't just recount the events, but that we truly evaluate the patterns.

QUESTION #2
How did it serve me?

Notice I didn't ask what the outcome was. Ever heard the phrase "it's better to be lucky than good?" Positive results do not always equate to positive experiences. We can get the result we want but go about it in ways that reinforce negative patterns. Remember the story from the last chapter of my son's hitting coach and what constitutes a great at-bat in baseball? Most people think that a successful at-bat in baseball is when they reach first base safely. However, if we change our perspective and consider the process of the at-bat and how I approached it, we broaden our perspective. It's not just about the outcome of a situation. It's about the process I used and the experience I had, irrespective of the outcome. This question is much the same.

When we ask if something serves us, we ask about the consequences of our actions on our behavior, well-being, relationships, and so on. For example, we might be on the fast track at work. Sure, the fast track comes with status and financial rewards. But there are costs to the fast track that might impact our personal life. Now, while this might be a cliched example, it highlights the nature of the question. It's not just about the outcome of one's actions. It's also about the costs and consequences of pursuing that outcome.

Answering this question is not trivial. It should not be done quickly. Or flippantly. It often requires very close, intentional support. The answers can stir emotions. They can challenge beliefs. They can disrupt patterns. But, if we can answer the question, we create both a deep awareness of the potentially negative results of our established patterns, as well as a sense of ownership to address them.

QUESTION #3
How might I do it differently?

If Question 2 is the most difficult, then Question 3 is the most fun. And, if we answer Question 2 with depth, we can approach Question 3 with expansion. And specificity. We begin to uncover several potential ways in which we can directly shift our behavior to change. I liken it to the quote from Michelangelo which started this chapter. If we can strip away the big blocks of stone that surround us, we can find the sculpture of our future self within, waiting to be revealed.

Equally important in answering this question is that we approach it with priority. Remember, we can't change everything at once. We should absolutely get as many ideas out as possible. But eventually, we need to bring a sense of priority to the shifts we believe have the most impact. If we can do so, that big list of things that want to change becomes one or two very clear dimensions of your behavior that you can focus on.

Let's try a little example.

If you haven't noticed by now, I can be a bit of a troublemaker. From a young age, I had a strong willingness to challenge authority. On more than one occasion in school, I got in trouble for challenging teachers. It often took the form of pointing out inconsistencies in arguments or lessons. One time, I outright addressed what I considered hypocrisy. Now, I was never rude. I would just . . . challenge.

This behavior followed me into my professional life. My intelligence and drive were strengths that led me to get opportunities. Once in organizations, particularly in hierarchical organizations. I would become frustrated. Frustrated with the "way things were." So, I would push. I pushed while at the Defense Intelligence Agency because an antiquated personnel system meant that I could not get promoted to a more senior pay rank, even though I was performing the duties of someone well beyond my years of experience. I was frustrated that the promotion system was based on "time-in-grade" instead of the meritocracy I thought it should be.

I recall similar feelings while at Booz Allen. After being promoted to Senior Associate, I had my eyes on the next level, Principal. I felt I was doing everything right to position myself. I recall bumping up against other leaders that were telling me, directly or indirectly, that I wasn't ready. After thirteen years at Booz Allen, I took a role with an English company, Smiths Group. Again, I pushed against some internal cultural aspects of the company that I felt were not in keeping with the modern work experience. At Ernst & Young (EY), I challenged the traditional partner promotion system. I was in a non-traditional, innovative role designed to launch new products and services (which I did quite successfully). Still, the organization wanted to "see more from me" before advancing me from Executive Director to Partner. I finally left for another Big Four consultancy, KPMG. And in two short years there, I managed to find myself leading an internal project across the firm and, once again, trying to get promoted to Partner outside the parameters of the established system.

With this context, let's return to the three questions.

QUESTION #1
How did I try to get promoted in the past?

Well, I pushed. I challenged the traditional structures in large, established companies with decades-long business models. I believed that the meritocracy of results was sufficient for the leaders around me to see that I was a different kind of leader, but one still worthy of the title of Partner. I was working hard. I was creating new services. Blazing new trails. All the while, I was challenging the organization in new ways. In effect, I was trying to get promoted by being the exception, not the rule.

QUESTION #2
How did that serve me?

The answer is—not great. I quickly developed a reputation for being impatient. While people appreciated my innovative, disruptive spirit, I was seen as someone who "didn't understand the nuances and subtleties of being a partner." I was considered someone who would occasionally not play the by the rules. Probably most harmfully, some thought I lacked the maturity to occupy the very role I was pursuing.

In this case, I didn't get promoted. Clearly. In my mind, I was filling the role that these firms hired me for: to be a dynamic leader capable of helping grow the business. Instead, I was, at times, doing quite the opposite. I was not building relationships that I needed to. I was not meeting the metrics leadership thought I should meet. It should be noted that I thought many of those metrics were silly. This should surprise no one. In short, my disruptive, authority challenging approach—an approach I was quite proud of—wasn't helping me at all. At least not in the way I was displaying it. Every strength is a weakness under the right conditions.

What's more, for a long while I never considered the idea that it was my fault. I found every reason in the book why the organization was to blame in some way. Poor leadership. Dumb metrics. Bad culture. Archaic business model. It wasn't until a coach of mine, a gentleman named Ken Durbin, to whom I'm forever indebted, gave me a piece of insight which stays with me to this day: "You have to be successful within the system in which you exist in order to change it." It was this piece of advice that changed my view forever.

QUESTION #3
How might I do it differently?

I learned two things from truly answering question two. First, the companies I worked for never asked me to be an internally disruptive force. They valued my brain and ability to create change, but they wanted that skill to be employed in the service of the company. Not in its disruption. Second, and most importantly, the one common denominator in every one of those experiences was . . . me.

If I were to be successful in my goal of becoming a partner, I would need to either change my approach or find a role in a company where my style was part of the job description. I needed to work harder to understand the spoken and unspoken rules of the road within my next company so that I could create the relationships and reputation necessary for leadership to see me as a worthy candidate. So, when I left KPMG for Prophet Brand Strategy, I did just that. I was hyperaware of my approach, my interactions, and of building relationships within the firm. Even then, I found myself quickly in the middle of trying to help, or push, this small consulting firm towards its goal of becoming a player in the large consulting market. And once again, I found that virtually no one who hired me into that firm had asked me to do so.

So, I finally learned my real lesson about what I needed to do differently. I started my own company.

FOUR PHASES TO SUCCESSFUL CHANGE

In the chapters that follow, I will give you a four-phased framework for how to build from these three questions to create your own change program. Where the three questions provide you a starting point to identify why and what to change, we still need to understand the how. And we already covered six strategies. You might think, "Wow. Three questions. Six strategies. Four phases. Michael, you're making this confusing!" Be not afraid.

The four phases will give you a structure to organize everything we've covered:

Phase 1—Reflect: In this phase, we ask and answer questions one and two. In this phase, we look deep into our history, preferences, patterns, and more, to understand how this thing called our brain has developed our own unique, never to be replicated by another human being, map of our own experience. And, most importantly, what happens as a consequence.

Phase 2—Shift: In this phase, we answer Question 3. We build from the insights gathered in the Reflect Phase to identify the superset of potential changes and, finally, the small number of critical changes that we need to make in our life.

Phase 3—Adopt: In this phase, we learn to implement the shifts we've identified. Drawing from the third principle outlined in Chapter 3, Initiate Movement, we'll test and learn from real-world experience. We'll draw from the other five principles to understand how creating small wins in the pursuit of our goals helps re-inform our understanding of why and what we need to change.

Phase 4—Adapt: In this phase, we draw from the lessons of Phase 3 to build a repeatable process that works to establish new, long-term patterns. In Phase 4, however, we don't just build the structures to address our identified shifts, we create an enduring capability for changing ourselves and a continuous loop of experience where we become truly adaptable. In doing so, we build the lifelong ability to change.

CHAPTER 9

Reflect

"Your vision will become clear only when you look into your own heart.
Who looks outside, dreams;
who looks inside, awakes."

CARL JUNG

T HIS IS, WITHOUT QUESTION, one of my favorite quotes. It's both inspiring and practical, with a hint of somberness. The simple message that *your vision lies within you* is central to the idea that the only person you can change is you. It also perfectly encapsulates the essence of the first step of change: Reflect. Many of us are quick to look outside ourselves to understand why we struggle or what stops us from achieving our goals. Certainly, there will always be external realities which shape our experience, but Dr. Jung reminds us of a fundamental truth—our true success lies in looking inward, not outward.

The Reflect Phase is the foundation of your change journey. Everything starts here. It is a phase that doesn't come with a pre-defined time window. It could take a day, a week, or a year. What's important is that the work is done to deeply understand our patterns and, most importantly, how those patterns have impacted us. It is often the case that we are unaware of the actions and events that lead us to our current reality. It's not that we are blissfully unaware. It's more that we are underinformed.

Recall from the research of Dr. Barrett that our brains are prediction machines. In the Reflect Phase, our goal is to look deep into those predictions based on our historical patterns and then to reframe our understanding of our current reality. If we are to follow Jung's advice, we must first look within.

Reflect serves another critically important purpose—to build the skill of evaluating and understanding our patterns. This is the critical skill required for us to change. The more we can self-identify negative behaviors and patterns, the more we can identify and design the solutions to them. Otherwise, the six strategies don't amount to much more than interesting science if we are unable to apply them. We must know and do. Like the Sistine Chapel, we must apply the science and create the artwork of our change story.

THE REFLECT PROCESS

First, let me say that I am not a big fan of processes. At least not linear ones. I don't believe people change in a linear fashion and therefore any prescribed linear process falls apart in the face of real human experience. But, for the purpose of helping you with your change journey, I understand processes must exist. My encouragement to you is that if a process step doesn't serve you, or you find that they are happening out of order, that's wonderful. Go with it. It's more than likely that you'll work in an iterative fashion through these experiences. But, since this is a book, we must go left to right and top to bottom—because we're working in two dimensions here. So, a sequence process it is.

Before we begin, let's remind ourselves of the key science strategies that play a large role in the Reflect Phase. These concepts include:

1. Our brains are prediction machines.

2. Our hormones influence our perception of the past, present, and future.

3. Our behavior patterns are created from long-term potentiation or long-term depression.

4. There is a difference between rewarding and reinforcing

behavior.

5. Errors are essential to trigger neuroplasticity.

6. We have two types of goals: approach and avoidance.

STEP 1
Audit Your Initial Change Goals

Note the word "initial." People often ask me how best to change. My response back to them is usually, "Well, that depends. What do you want to change?" I get a lot of different answers. Some specific. Most tend to be general. Be better at X. Do more of Y. Do less of Z. Sometimes all of them together. But, more often than not, what they start with is not what they end with. And that is because of the Reflect Phase. But we must start here, nonetheless.

The first step is to simply write down all the things you want to change. In no particular order, simply list them. Turns out that the sequence you list them in tends to be what you inherently view as the most important anyway. But just write them down. You can do this alone or with some help. Then, for each thing you want to change, identify if this is an "Approach" goal, i.e., something you want to do more of, or if it is an "Avoidance" goal, i.e., something you want to do less of. When you're done, add up the number of Approach goals and the number of Avoidance goals. This is the first pattern we can observe about how we perceive change.

This is not some judgement that having more Approach goals is better than having more Avoidance goals. There is no inherent value in either. But we might infer certain tendencies as a result of having more of one type. Having a preponderance of approach goals may signal a certain dissatisfaction with your current circumstances. You may also be someone who has grand plans, but you aren't quite able to put those plans into action. Because of this, your list of things you want to go do continues to grow. Having a majority of avoidance goals could signal a struggle with behavioral control. Perhaps you're someone who struggles to break old habits. There are many reasons why you might find yourself with more of one type. For many people, for example, health goals tend to be more easily identified as Avoidance goals (e.g., lose weight, drink less, don't eat junk food). This is largely because we more easily see the effects of our negative behaviors. Professional goals, in contrast, tend to feel more Approach-like. Goals such as making more money, getting a promotion, and changing careers all reflect a future-focused orientation that is characterized as pursuing or attaining something new. By categorizing your initial list of change goals this way, you will be able to get a big picture view. Perhaps just that list alone will give you an insight that you previously did not have.

Interestingly, it might also signal where you are having success. Having fewer avoidance goals might indicate that you have an effective framework for reducing unwanted behaviors. Having a smaller approach goal list might mean you've accomplished many of your larger goals, but perhaps those have come at a cost in other areas of your life.

Step 2
Cluster and Prioritize

Now it's time to organize your initial goals into similar categories, for example relationships, health, career, finances, and so on. Again, there's no secret to the categories here. Whatever makes sense to you. This gives you a secondary view of your initial change goals, now organized by the most important topics. What you'll now be able to see is 1) how many change goals do you have in similar areas? And, 2) within each category, do you have mostly approach goals or avoidance goals?

The trick now is to whittle this larger list down to no more than three change objectives you wish to pursue. The first two steps of this process bring a bit of structure to organizing your initial thoughts. This should inform your selection of the three most important objectives. You might start with a "most to least important" hierarchy of your categories. Another common way to prioritize within a list is to assign points to each of your key categories. For example, you can assign ten points total across your five categories. Health might receive five points because it's your primary focus. This would leave you with five points to assign across relationships, career, and financial. A tournament-style process can also be fun. In this example, you pit two categories against each other and "pick the winner" through a series of pairwise matchups. For example, between Health and Finances, I would choose Health. Between Relationships and Health, I might still choose Health. Then between Finances and Relationships I would pick Relationships. The result would be a list of my most important priorities—Health first, Relationships second, and Finances third.

But this is also where the art of transformation comes in. What is most important for you might not be the area that has the greatest number of change goals. It might be the area in your life where you're experiencing the most friction. Here's a little trick to help you if you're stuck. Ask other people. Sharing your list of objectives with others, as well as how you've organized it, is a fantastic way to get new input. Remember, your brain is a prediction machine based on your own unique experience. There's a bit of circular logic to the idea that each of us can pick the best change path for ourselves based on the patterns we've historically built. After all, how can you decide what you need to change if what you need to change is a function of what you haven't changed so far? Share your list. Ask for input. Be vulnerable with people you trust. Even consider asking people you don't know well who can share new ideas. An example might be a coworker or professional peer that you only occasionally interact with. I've often asked close friends or professional connections to introduce me to someone they know well, but I don't. In this case, I know it's someone that comes with an endorsement of a trusted source but doesn't have history with me directly.

What should remain at the end of this process is the, at most, three change objectives you want to focus on. An example of how to Cluster and Prioritize is below.

CLUSTER

Health	Career	Relationships
1. Lose 20 pounds (Avoid)	1. Get promoted (Approach)	1. Be more present for family (Approach)
2. Lower my cholesterol (Avoid)	2. Work less on weekends (Avoid)	2. Take two trips per year (Approach)
3. Eat less junk food (Avoid)	3. Be a better manager (Approach)	3. Be more patient (Approach)

APPROACH GOALS = 5   AVOIDANCE GOALS = 4

PRIORITIZE

Approach	Avoidance
1. Get promoted (Career)	1. Lose 20 pounds (Health)
2. Be more present for family (Relationships)	2. Work less on weekends (Relationships)
3. Be more patient (Relationships)	3. Lower my cholesterol (Health)
4. Take two trips per year (Relationships)	4. East less junk food (Health)
5. Be a better manager (Career)	

STEP 3
Audit My Approach

Now that you've selected three goals, we must begin the process of evaluating the behavior patterns we have created. In Chapter 8, I shared the three questions that can change your life. Step 3 is about the first question: "How have I tried to approach this goal in the past?" I provided an example from my life about how to answer those questions.

Now you might be thinking to yourself, "Well, I have an approach goal to start my own company, and I've never tried that before. That's why it's a goal!" If this were the case, the question should prompt you to ask, "Why haven't I tried it before?" In my case, I was resting on the safety of a large company because of the fear of the financial instability that comes with entrepreneurship. So, my approach was to try to be disruptive within an established company to scratch my innovation itch while still playing it safe. After several failed attempts, I learned it wasn't possible to have both. At least not how I was approaching it. In short, if you've attempted to make this change before and have not been successful, why? If you haven't tried, why?

The answer to this question should cover a number of items. Again, there are no hard and fast rules here. But here are things to cover to the best of your abilities:

- The number of times you've tried to make the change previously.

- How long it's been since the last time you attempted.

- The steps you took, particularly if they were the same each time or changed.

- The circumstances of your life at the time you attempted the change.

- Any support you had. Or didn't have.

What you want to cover are both the steps you've taken and the conditions around you as you took them. Your approach to this question can be fairly clinical at this point. It helps to ask others who might have experienced you during this time to share their perceptions of how you approached the situation. Again, the input of others is a great buffer against your own unique brain telling your own story and then predicting your future.

Step 4
Audit My Experience

Now the second question: "How did it serve me?" This is, without question, the most difficult question to answer. As I mentioned in example in Chapter 8, this question can stir emotions. Depending on the topic, it can require the support of a trained professional. If you need this kind of help, please get it. Committing to this process requires that we, as Dr. Jung observed, go within ourselves. Because, if the only person you can change is yourself, then you must deeply understand how your actions, or inactions, behaviors, and beliefs, created the reality in which you find yourself today. Again, each of us is affected by external events and circumstances that can have large consequences on our lives and our ability to change. But, to use another of my favorite quotes from Charles Swindoll, "Life is 10% what happens to you and 90% how you react to it." Our goal here is to deeply understand that 90%.

One method for quickly identifying the impacts from your historical approach is to revisit the prioritization of your categories from Step 2. For example, if you've identified "relationships" as your most important category—begin by evaluating the impact of your previous actions on the important relationships in your life. You might have indicated that relationships are important, but when you look at your historical actions, you might have prioritized other areas of your life and, as a result, have experienced negative relationship impacts. This effectively compares your stated level of importance with your actions. I put the insights garnered from this evaluation into the "unintended consequences" bucket.

This step also requires that you ask yourself how you felt, or feel, as it relates to your change objective. If you've made attempts at change in the past, how did you feel during those attempts? If you wanted to start your own company, what did the experience of working in a corporate job feel like? Was it a grind? Did you struggle to maintain motivation day in and day out? Did you feel like you were "missing something" or not living your full purpose? Perhaps you've been wanting to make a healthy lifestyle change. How did it feel when you made attempts in the past? Were you frustrated? How did you handle that frustration? What kept you motivated? Why did you stop?

This step is another great opportunity for feedback from others. Questions such as "Did I seem happy?", "What was it like to interact with me?", "Did you notice anything specific about me during that time?" These are questions that help overcome your brain's unique map and predictions by including feedback from others.

It is also a great way to help you uncover previously missed errors. Remember, errors signal to the brain that something needs to change. Errors don't just have to happen in real time. Recall that we humans have the unique ability to understand the past. And, because learning occurs through repetition, if we can identify negative patterns that have repeatedly occurred, we are actively signaling to our brains today that change is required.

Step 5
Revisiting my change goals

I often tell my clients that I like to Jedi-mind trick them. Sometimes it's in a coaching capacity. Sometimes it's in a workshop. I also like to tell them they will get very frustrated with me and this process. Truth in advertising. But I need to admit something to you. I've been Jedi mind tricking you. It's not that steps 1 through 4 aren't the process. Of course they are. But what you've been reading is a series of steps that seem logical. Make a list. Review the list. Prioritize the list. Analyze the list. Pick from the list. While these are all true, there's a more important thing happening beneath the surface: You are rebuilding your brain's prediction machine by challenging your beliefs. You are fundamentally asking yourself, "Why do I want the things I want?" Or "Are the things I want *really* the things I want?" Most importantly, you're asking yourself, "Why should I believe my brain?" These are the foundations of change.

Steps 1-4 are all designed to support Step 5, which is about triggering the neuroplasticity needed to signal a change is needed. Ironically, however, it often turns out not to be the change we originally defined in Step 1. That's why I used the word "initial." Remember, our patterns are created through repetition (long-term potentiation) or by inaction (long-term depression). When we identify those patterns and the errors that have held us back from achieving our goals, we get a much different view of what's required for change. And, often, a complete revision of the change goals that we started with.

There's another important thing happening. We are parsing through two types of behaviors we've already discussed: rewarding and reinforcing behaviors. Many of our goals exist because we value, or want to acquire, the rewards of change. But we fail at change because we struggle to execute the positive reinforcing behaviors necessary to get the rewards. What we have been doing in steps 1-4 is, without specifically labeling them, identifying those behaviors. Now, it's not always the case that you will change your goal. It may still be something you desire to change. But what you should uncover are the specific behaviors you need to change in order to accomplish that goal. Remember, we control the inputs and actions (or verbs) to change. We don't always control the outcome. Like my son's hitting coach, we must understand what's keeping me from getting a "good at bat" every time.

A CASE STUDY ILLUSTRATION

With one of my large clients, I had been working with a cohort of senior managers to improve their level of empowerment in the business. As a fairly hierarchical company, a long history of top-down management had left the middle leadership layer somewhat atrophied. Those leaders tended to wait for instructions and/or need to get approval from their director-level leaders before taking action. This slowed down decision-making and stifled creativity.

One of those senior managers, James, was working with me in a coaching capacity. James told me he was planning to retire in five to seven years, and he was looking to get promoted to director before that. He had a set of financial goals for him and his family and becoming director would substantially improve his plans for retirement. Through our discussions, I learned he had a couple of "passion-projects" that he and his wife had been curating for years. One of them, a retreat-style spa experience, was what he explained they would focus on after he left the company.

James is an outstanding engineer. He's hardworking and comes to work with a focus on creating value in the organization. He's efficient, diligent, and respectful of his leadership's time. As a result, James tends to be pretty matter of fact. Out of deference to his leaders, he ensures that he minimizes disruption to their time, specifically cutting out any unnecessary socialization they might deem "a waste of time."

As I worked with James, he mentioned he had applied for over twenty director-level positions during his time at the company. As one might expect, he had grown disenfranchised and demotivated by his several failed attempts. James mentioned that it felt like the people who got the jobs weren't always qualified but were, "the friends of the leaders and the people they liked best."

Clearly, James' change goal was to get promoted. A new director position had opened, and he was planning to apply. As we explored the new position, I asked him question 1: "How have you approached promotion opportunities in the past?" James recounted that he'd taken his very business-like approach. He acknowledged he was keeping his personality lowkey and focused all his interactions on business matters in the most efficient way possible. He focused heavily on his technical credibility. As you can imagine, when I asked him question 2: "How did that serve you?" his answer was, "Well I haven't been promoted, so . . ." So, we dug a little deeper. I acknowledged that not getting promoted was the outcome, but I asked him about the experience. He, of course, outlined his disappointment, but as we spoke, he described this idea of "not being himself." He said he wasn't the same person at work that he was outside of work, that he felt like he had to censor himself to fit into the culture. More importantly, he said he felt as if no one knew the real him. He questioned why he was even there in the first place.

James realized that the story he'd been telling himself about how to show up at work wasn't serving him. Not only was it not resulting in getting promoted, but it was resulting in a form of personal censorship that he was only recently aware of. What started as a goal of getting promoted turned into a realization that the change he needed to make was to be his authentic self. He had been changing his behavior for years to receive validation from others. The change that needed to be made was inside James, in his behaviors and thoughts about his inherent value. I recall sharing a story with James about how badly I wanted to make partner at my previous companies. Once I made it, I realized that isn't really what I had wanted. What I was struggling with was my own inherent sense of value, and I was using a title as validation. In both our cases, the promotion was the "rewarding behavior" we sought.

Much like I realized, James realized he needed to make a shift. The organization didn't need to make a shift. He did. And that shift is the next phase of the change process.

CHAPTER 10

Shift

"The optimist sees the donut; the pessimist sees the hole."
FLORENCE McLANDBURGH

I N 2020, *NEW YORK TIMES* best-selling author Bruce Feiler wrote a book called *Life is in the Transitions*. Inspired by some of his, and his father's, own ongoing life challenges, Bruce embarked on a three-year journey to interview over 200 people about the biggest transitions of their lives. What resulted was an incredibly rich and moving tapestry of stories about everyday people managing the most difficult, life-altering transitions of their lives. Transitions that often shook the foundation of their very identity. It is a wonderful read and deeply insightful. I suggest you give it a read.

Without spoiling the details, there is an important theme to Bruce's work. Bruce identifies fifty-two different types of transitions across five categories: body, love, work, identity, and beliefs. However, the vast majority of these life transitions were unexpected. They were things that happened to people. Or, by contrast, things that happened deeply within them, things such as core religious beliefs or sexual identity, that were core to who there are as people. We all are faced at various times in our life with these kinds of macro changes which we have to face. If you're facing one of those, you'll find comfort and tools within Bruce's work.

Here in the Shift Phase, we are operating at a layer below life-altering transitions. Having said that, if you can build the ability to *shift*, you'll be able to weather those life-altering transitions much more capably than many. In the stories that Bruce shares, people are thrust into a new perspective because the circumstances of their life change dramatically. What we are talking about here is the everyday change that we prompt through the deep insights gained in the Reflect phase. It's the change we know we must do, but haven't done, or are afraid to do.

Through all my work with organizations, teams, and individuals, I've noticed something. We tend to be, not always, better at corrective behavior than we are at preventative behavior. It's easier to fix a problem we can all see than it is to prevent that problem from ever happening. We can struggle with the return-on-investment (ROI) for something that perhaps never happens. Now, this isn't some commentary on the decaying moral fabric of a society that can't delay gratification. It is true that many of our habits and behaviors are rooted in a much more near-term orientation. As we learned, effort must be the reward of our goal pursuit. One of my favorite phrases from James Clear's *Atomic Habits* perfectly encapsulates this idea: "The costs of our good habits are in the present. The costs of our poor habits are in the future."

Which is why shifting, not just our perspective, but also the language we give to our goals, is so important. We know errors signal to the brain that a change is needed. Understanding this, if we are better at corrective behavior, i.e., fixing problems, we can leverage this tendency to rebuild our perspective around what needs to change. And this is what Shift is about. It's about reframing our goals and giving a new language to our focus. In Bruce's work, it was clear to the people he interviewed what needed to change. Life sort of hit them in the face with it. But in our everyday lives, these changes are not always as clear. In this phase, we'll identify that change and, in doing so, bring the focus we need for our change efforts.

THE SHIFT PROCESS

As we did with Reflect, let's review briefly a few of the key scientific principles that play a large role in the Shift Phase. You will note as we progress through each of the phases, many of these principles align to more than one phase. While there are areas where one principle may be a more significant component of the process, these principles work horizontally across multiple areas of the change process. Specifically, the principles relevant to the Shift Phase are:

1. Our Brains are Prediction Machines: Our exploration is limited by our experience.

2. Create Focus: We need alertness, energy, and attention to change. Most of all, we must decision what behavior we want to "unlearn."

3. The Science of Motivation: How we design and pursue our goals influences our motivation levels. Motivation is heavily tied to our visual system and the experience of pursuit. Motivation is the fuel that moves us from habit to change.

4. Approach vs Avoidance Goals: We are more motivated by goals we pursue than behaviors we try to avoid.

5. The Importance of Errors: Errors signal to the brain that something must be corrected and opens the opportunity for neuroplasticity.

6. Learning: To learn anything we need alertness, energy, and attention. As well as deciding what to unlearn.

7. Mindsets: A "Stress-is-enhancing" and "growth mindset" are critical elements of reframing our goal perspective and experience of stress.

STEP 1
Shifting Perspective

In Chapter 8, I introduced the three questions that can change your life. We covered the first two of those in the Reflect phase. We begin the Shift phase by addressing the last question: "How might I do it [whatever I want to change] differently?" Recall that what we should have brought with us into the Shift phase three change goals that we explored in the Reflect phase. At the end of Reflect, we looked at these three areas and evaluated how we've approached these goals in the past, if at all, and explored how that approach served us. We looked at both the outcomes and the experience. In doing so, we signaled our brains, through the identification of errors in our approach, that something needed to change. That we need to change. And here we get to explore, to what new end.

In classic brainstorming fashion, we get to explore all the ways we might correct our historical approach. There are countless ways to brainstorm this. Keep a running list. Work with a friend or peer. Heck, you could throw your Reflect results into ChatGPT and ask for five ways you could approach a specific situation differently. There is no right answer here. Except for one thing. You must recognize that the same brain you used to get you into this situation is the same brain you're asking to devise a different approach. This isn't to say that your brain can't devise a different approach, it's to acknowledge that your brain is likely going to have gaps because you have strongly established habits and patterns. After all, remember that our brains are prediction machines. If you want to start with a list you generate, that's fine, but get that list in front of other people. You need feedback, perspective, and information outside of yourself to truly explore the wealth of possibilities.

I would recommend you talk to as many people as you can. Recall from the example in Chapter 9 that James had been taking a similar approach when applying for promotion roles. He repeated the same action again and again, to the point where his conclusion was that he hadn't been efficient and competent enough. He needed to double down on his business-like approach. Through exploration with me, what he realized is that he needed to show up differently. He needed to be his authentic self. His brain's prediction machine couldn't have imagined that a different approach was required.

Here's a cheat code for how you know you're getting close to the right shift. It scares you. Or it makes you say, "Oh, I don't think I could do that." Any appropriately semi-terrified response will do. The idea here is not to trust the story your brain is telling you. That's the brain that got you into this situation. Of course, there are measures of risk, financial realities, etc. that prevent an unlimited, unrestricted response. But if your solution doesn't make the stress response start to trigger, you're not shooting far enough.

STEP 2
The From-To Statement

The way you capture your shift is in a From-To statement. A From-To statement is a simple phrase that does what the name implies. It describes the behavior I'm moving away from and then the behavior I'm moving to. A simple example could be "I am going from dedicating all my time to others each day to reserving at least one hour of time for self-care every day." Now, you might think that's not terrifying. But imagine an overburdened, working parent with small children who is trying to do it all and struggles with extreme guilt any time they spend time on themselves. You better believe that is scary. They might have their family conditioned to expect their full attention at all times. Some people might have to hear the word "no" more than they are used to.

A From-To statement should be sufficiently clear enough that someone who doesn't know you can understand exactly what change is occurring. The From component is a direct result of the work you did in Reflect. The To statement is the articulation of the approach goal that resulted from your exploration and feedback in Step 1. An example of a From-To statement from a recent coaching client of mine who was struggling with delegation was "I intended to shift from being the single point of failure for my department to delegating and empowering my team to lead and deliver." This was a huge move for them. This is a big task for many. What was particularly effective in this statement was the phrase "being the single point of failure." This is a tough phrase. But through deep work in the Reflect phase, they identified that this was indeed the case. The To component "delegating and empowering" was sufficient to identify the preferred behavior and why that behavior was important.

So, why do we do this? Recall that errors trigger neuroplasticity. When we are clear about the From condition we are trying to correct, we clearly focus the brain on what needs to change. In addition, since we tend to be a bit better at corrective behavior than preventative behavior, we lean into that tendency more clearly. More specifically, remember the distinction of reinforcing and rewarding behavior? When we address the *From* condition clearly, we are often identifying the root cause of the reinforcing behavior that is holding us back. For example, we might say, "I want to shift *from* being someone who procrastinates to being someone who takes proactive steps, even if small, towards my goals." In this case, we've identified procrastination as the reinforcing behavior. We procrastinate, even though we know it's not particularly helpful in achieving our goals. Remember, a reinforcing behavior is simply a trigger or action that we want to repeat. In this case, we've indicated that we want to replace procrastination with taking proactive steps, because making progress towards my goals is rewarding. Recall that our brain's greatest dopamine response comes through striving. So, when we redefine a *To* condition in this manner, we direct the brain towards pursuit—a critical component to motivation.

Writing these down has another important benefit. It alerts others to the changes you're making. In doing so, we give both a language, meaning we define the change, but we also give a measure of accountability to ourselves. After all, if someone close to me saw I was procrastinating, they only needed to refer me back to my From-To statement to highlight where my focus should be. Remember, we are a social species and engaging in social behavior is the among the most biologically rewarding actions we can take.

Writing a From-To statement is an artform. While we can leverage the scientific principles above, designing a From-To statement that works for you is going to be uniquely yours. Your statement won't necessarily be one that works for anyone else. The goal is to be specific enough that you can identify the change, but not so specific that you limit your ability to experiment with the changes you're trying to make. We'll explore this idea more in the next chapter. The statement should be clear, but not overly specific. For example, the To statement shouldn't be something you'll only have to do once to be successful. However, the statement can't be so vague that it lets you off the hook for accomplishing something. For example, a From-To statement that says, "I want to shift from being selfish to being a better person," while certainly a positive change, is much too broad. If I were working with an individual with this initial statement, we'd spend time being more specific about what "being a better person" actually means, then doing our best to include that in the To. My recommendation is to experiment with a few statements and then share them with others to get feedback.

STEP 3
Motivation and Mindset

If you recall from Chapter 3, Initiative Movement, one of the ways in which we can spike our motivation is to redefine the start of our journey as a goal. At least the first goal. This should be no different. Completing your From-To statements is a huge accomplishment. Writing them down is not just the beginning of your change journey. It's the completion of your specific articulation of the behaviors you want to change. You should have three new approach goals articulated in a From-To format. You've done an incredible amount of work to get to this point. While it might seem like nothing more than a few statements, recall that you've spent a considerable amount of time reflecting on your historical behavior, as well as redefining your goals. This should spike your dopamine and, as a result, your motivation.

This is a good place to make a point about your From-To statements. They should scare you. At least a little. These should not be small adjustments. Sure, there are levels to this and within the two-to-three that you selected, there can be some that are more difficult than others. This entire book is about change. Real, not superficial, change. If your brain is anything like the rest of humanity, and it is, something else will now happen. You'll look at each of these From-To statements and think, "Oh, man. Now I have to do this."

The intersection of this experience might feel a bit like the moment you're ascending on a roller coaster before the steep drop. Remember, the stress response is generic. The magnitude of the change before you will trigger stress, which will release cortisol, and the anticipation of pursuing your goals will release dopamine. An internal struggle will ensure. The closer the roller coaster gets to the crest of the drop, the higher the anticipation. And stress. It is this same experience that creates the focus we need for change.

This is the moment to enlist our combined stress-is-enhancing and growth mindset. It might be tempting to look at your new goals and think "it's just too much." At our disposal are science-backed strategies to change our perspective about this experience. This is, in fact, our first opportunity to practice the art of change. Pushing through this anxiety and not listening to your brain's prediction is your next opportunity for change. Irrespective of what your From-To statement says, you will have some version of this experience. Your task is to press forward. Acknowledging that you're stressed and that you're unsure of your ability to make the changes that are needed is perfectly normal. In fact, it's required. Your choice to press forward, to consciously decide that you will continue on despite those feelings, is exactly the kind of experience your anterior mid-cingulate cortex (aMCC) needs. And it's the important first step on your change journey.

STEP 4
Deciding What to Give Up

There's one last item to write down. And that is what you plan to give up. The From condition is the identification of the old behavior we want to change. Clearly, that's something we'll be trading in for our new behavior. But what we are talking about here is something different. You must decide what you are going to give up on the path to the new behavior. Our From-To statement has all the essential ingredients for learning. One, it identifies the errors we've made to trigger neuroplasticity. Two, it creates enough stress to create the alertness (i.e., focus) we need to learn something new. And three, it's specific in what I need to focus on (i.e. attention). The last piece is the conscious choice of what you want to unlearn to create space for that new behavior. Recall that to learn something new, you need to be clear about what you plan to give up.

The importance of writing this down is that it creates a similar focus as your From-To statement. This doesn't need to be the Anti-Vision Board of Bad Behavior. It simply must be a conscious acknowledgement of what you will not do in favor of what you will do. A simple example is something like giving up alcohol to support a healthier lifestyle. There are other less obvious things such as not speaking first in a meeting, not assuming you know what someone is thinking, or trusting your initial emotional reaction. We are not trying to create a new avoidance goal here. Our *To* statement is our approach goal. We are simply acknowledging that in order to realize the new *To* we must make a trade. Writing it down has the added benefit of creating alertness and awareness, which helps you recognize when you're doing the thing you don't want to do. By the way, here's a good little cheat code for what you have to give up . . . it is likely one of your habits. If it wasn't, you wouldn't have built a From-To statement for it in the first place.

A CASE STUDY ILLUSTRATION

One of my clients was a large technology company that had risen from the early days of a start-up to a full-fledged public company. I've seen this in other technology companies—and it was certainly true here—that much of the scrappy, get-it-done mindset that characterizes startups often carries on well into the company's growth. This is particularly true of founders. In the early days of the company's existence, two things determined its success: the quality of the technology and the resilience of the team. Both perfectly understandable traits.

By the time I arrived to help the company, they were well into the thousands of employees. However, much of the original leadership team remained. As the company grew, many of the leaders who assumed senior manager, director, or vice president positions tended to (no surprise) have similar characteristics as the founder. Deep technical expertise, as well as a predisposition towards perseverance over process. There was little process discipline or governance in the company. It had become just a big startup.

The challenge in these organizations is that at some point leaders need to shift from being responsible for the work and technology to being responsible for the people. This was the problem for one of my clients, an IT Director, Anthony. Anthony was a rising star. Not only was he an incredible programmer, he also had a strong business sense and was instrumental in several of the early innovations that helped move the company forward.

But Anthony struggled to teach and mentor his team. I call this the "player-to-coach" challenge. Like many others, Anthony was promoted because of his skills and productivity. He had a hard time teaching others to do what he did. This meant he ended up taking on more and more of the work. Which left little time for managing the team. It didn't lead to productivity challenges, however. Why? Well, because Anthony hired people with strong technical skills. After all, that's what Anthony had. Instead, it led to quality issues and late delivery because the team wasn't aligned.

In my work with Anthony, he discovered he had been valuing technical skills over everything else. As he told stories, he used phrases like "I got burned" or "that person didn't work out" to describe people he had hired. He said, "It's frustrating to have to explain everything, so it's just easier to do the work myself. It's faster and I know it will be done right." You can imagine that in his answers to the first two questions, "How have I done [something] in the past?" and "How did it serve me?", we uncovered a fear of relinquishing control.

After much work, he arrived at his From-To Statement. "I must shift from doing all the work and being afraid to let go of control to teaching and trusting my team." Similar to the example earlier about being a single point of failure (I see this a lot), Anthony decided to include the phrase "afraid to let go." This was a bold move. One that he admitted to me was not his traditional approach and one that he was incredibly nervous about. He had been doing things this way for a long, long time. The inclusion of "trusting and teaching" was specifically included. It wasn't that he just needed to let go, he needed to teach his team. This implies a dedication of time away from doing the work himself to helping others learn how to do the work. He needed to shift from being the player to being the coach.

Anthony had all the right components in his From-To statement. One, he identified the error he had made previously, which was doing all the work himself. Two, he defined and approached goals built on trusting and teaching his team, which gave him a clear focus. Three, it was sufficiently scary that it triggered alertness via the stress response. And four, he identified what he needed to give up: control. He had built up, and was rewarded for, his habit of being a productive programmer. It was going to take him more time now to teach his team. Time he otherwise would have spent doing the work.

Anthony also did one last thing. He shared his From-To statement with his team and with his vice president. In doing so, he put himself on notice. Not only did he signal that he had done the work to reflect on what needed to change, but he created an expectation from those around him that he would work on it. He didn't say he would be perfect. But it gave his change goal a clear language that others could identify.

This was not an inconsequential shift for him. Through hard work, he clearly identified what needed to change. But, as I've mentioned, knowing is not the same as doing. Change is an applied science. Anthony needed to put his shift into motion. He was ready for phase three. And so are you.

CHAPTER 11

Adopt

"It's easier to act your way into a new way of thinking,
than think your way into a new way of acting."
JERRY STERNIN

A
T THE END OF CHAPTER 1, I wrote about mindset. If you think about that section and read the quote above, you might find yourself noting a contradiction. "Michael, you just said that we need to have a stress-is-enhancing and growth mindset, but the quote above says that we need to act our way into a new way of thinking." I want to be clear about something. Mindset is a tool we use to navigate the hardships, obstacles, and stresses of change. Mindset is not manifesting. You cannot manifest your way into a new you. You have to act your way into a new you. A stress-is-enhancing and growth mindset supports your journey to act in new ways. Mindset alone is not enough. It must be matched with action.

Now that we've gotten that out of the way, this is one of my favorite quotes. I use it in workshops, presentations, coaching sessions, and more. I love it because I believe it speaks to the action-oriented and personal nature of change. It also implies another essential element of change—teaching our brain something new. We teach our brain something new by trying new things in new ways. The only way we can change our prediction machine is to give that machine new experiences. In Reflect and Shift, we analyzed our patterns and redefined our goals. In this phase we initiate movement and act.

Our goal here is simple—to test the new behaviors and changes we identified in Shift so we can 1) learn what works for us and 2) give our brain new experiences. This is the phase where we gather practical, real-world experiences, observations, and feedback. It is also the phase where we make errors. Recall that errors signal our brain that a change is needed. By this point, you've spent time describing the errors of the past. This is the point when we test and learn. Most importantly, it's the phase when we begin the process of breaking habits. Habits and behaviors we determined are holding us back.

THE ADOPT PROCESS

As the Adopt Phase is about action, we lean heavily on the six science-backed strategies to bring this phase to life. Among the critical elements of this phase are:

1. Initiate Movement—Apply strategies for managing our motivation to move forward into uncertainty.

2. Embrace Stress—Apply strategies for rebuilding our relationship with stress to manage the complex, uncomfortable emotions involved with change.

3. Shift Environment—Shift your environment to create constraints and to access your desired behaviors.

4. Generate Repetitions—Execute the actions of change, make errors, and collect feedback to update your approach.

5. Reward Progress—Focus on the effort, not outcome, of change. Identify and measure the inputs (e.g., actions) that create movement in the direction of your change goals.

6. The Science of Doing Hard Things—Train your anterior Mid-Cingulate Cortex (aMCC) through intentional participation in difficult activities that trigger neuroplasticity.

STEP 1
Identify your verbs

Notice at the end of Shift we did not identify a quantitative target for your shift. That is purposeful. Remember that effort is the reward of change. We must focus on the input required to create change. Our only goal in the Adopt phase is to *try* to change. It is not to change. That might sound confusing. Let me give an example. Many people have a goal of losing weight. When they set that goal, they will identify an amount of weight to lose. For the next several weeks, they stand on the scale every morning to see their progress. Inevitably, the scale barely moves each day. In some cases, it might go up. Instead, if my goal is to lose weight, what I need to measure are the actions that I take to lose weight. For example, I would work out for thirty minutes a day, four days a week, for one month. I would track the number of times that I completed that thirty-minute session. Perhaps I'm looking to make a career change. My action might be to submit to five jobs per week. If my shift were to dedicate more time to self-care without feeling guilty, my first action would be to set aside the dedicated time each week. That's the first verb to track.

The value of this kind of initial tracking is that it is a binary goal. I don't have to worry about what the scale will say in the morning. I just complete the thirty-minute workout today. Either I did it, or I didn't. In addition, remember that we struggle with evaluating the time required to accomplish our goals. This is the prospective time problem. We struggle to maintain motivation for goals that are far into the distance. But, four thirty-minute sessions this week? Well, that's easy to track, and when I complete those four sessions, I receive a dopamine response associated with accomplishing my four-part goal. Breaking up your actions in this manner also helps with the messy middle problem of goal pursuit that we identified in Chapter 3.

Let's say my goal is more behavioral in nature and not physical. Perhaps my shift was to delegate more work, like we saw from Anthony in Chapter 10. What verbs would he track? One might be the number of times he simply delegated work. But another might be the number of coaching sessions he performed with his team. The more he teaches his team, the more he's able to trust their work. So, instead of simply tracking the total volume of work he's delegated, he should track the frequency with which he delegates and teaches. The more he does that, the more it becomes a habit and, eventually, more work will be delegated.

STEP 2
Design your timeline

Once you have your verbs, you need to set a timeline. Remember, this phase is called Adopt. That means we only need to identify a window in which we plan to perform our verbs. The timeline must be long enough to execute enough attempts at the new behavior to observe yourself and gather feedback. Since we know we struggle with understanding the distance to our goals, your focus here is to create a series of time windows that coincide with your verbs. I encourage the Day-Week-Month format. There are two ways to implement it.

Approach One: Total Effort Count

- Day: the time dedicated to the change effort per day (e.g., ten minutes of meditation).

- Week: the number of days per week you plan to dedicate to the effort.

- Month: Number of days per month as a result of the days plus weeks goal.

The value of this approach is that you break the larger set of effort into smaller chunks. This helps with multiple motivation points, as well as managing the messy middle of goal pursuit. It helps me narrow my focus on the daily goal while creating incremental progress.

Approach Two: Effort Variation

- Day: an effort goal I commit to perform on a daily basis (e.g., fifteen-minute journaling)

- Week: an effort goal that I commit to doing at least once per week (e.g., one hour of uninterrupted self-care time)

- Month: an effort goal that I commit to doing at least once per month (e.g., leave work early to spend time with my spouse).

In contrast to the first approach, this allows you to vary the effort goal to practice more behaviors, but limit the number of times you perform them. You pick an effort goal that you can do every day. Then, a different goal that you commit to once per week. You get to pick the day. Then, pick a goal you perform once per month. The idea here, however, is that the goals should be commensurate in effort for the time interval. If you're only doing something once per month, the effort should be more intense. The downside, of course, is that you don't make as many attempts at the same effort. But the diversity of goals can help with motivation.

With either approach, you should not go beyond two months. The goal here is to test and learn. We'll set longer timelines in the next phase.

STEP 3
Generate repetitions

Now that you have a timeline, you must act on it as much as you possibly can. And, perhaps more importantly, you must make errors. The strategies for this step are outlined in depth in Chapter 6. Because we are focused on effort repetitions at this point, your approach to the effort can, and should, vary. What matters is that you complete the effort. By varying your approach to the effort, you expand your range of available feedback and observation. For example, perhaps your shift goal is to increase your knowledge of financial health and wellness. One day you might dedicate thirty minutes to online training and learning. The next thirty-minute effort might be trying to re-teach that material to your spouse. The next thirty-minute effort might be to work with a financial coach.

There's one thing I'll add. Do something physically demanding that isn't associated with your goal. This could be a cold shower, a fifteen-minute workout, a focused meditation session, etc. Within the safe capacity of your physical ability (and maybe slightly beyond), complement your behavior efforts with physical effort. If you can combine them, even better. I often listen to books and podcasts while I run. Without any other distractions, other than my fatigue, I can create focused learning.

The audio distracts me from being tired and narrows my mental focus. Recall that we must create focus in order to learn. A physical stimulus in advance of our effort attempts will create the alertness, energy, and attention we need.

STEP 4
Document your observations

One habit you'll need to develop, irrespective of your shift goal, is the ability to observe and assess your behavior. It is certainly helpful to have feedback from others, and we'll do that here, but your ability to not just act, but to also observe yourself, is critical. As I work with many of my clients, you must develop the ability to evaluate not just what you did, but also how you did it. We started building that muscle in the Reflect Phase. Think of this step as a miniature version of that experience. There's a difference here, however. In the Reflect Phase, we spent time evaluating a long-established pattern of behavior. In this case, we'll have a smaller sample size of new behaviors that, by definition, will all feel foreign. The trick, of course, is not to associate that foreignness with negativity. Here's how you do that.

1. Observing Reactions in Yourself: Imagine the anxiety you feel before having a hard discussion with your spouse. Then think about how you feel after that is done. It's usually very different. I often say that the conversation I have with myself before a two-minute cold shower is very different from the conversation I have with myself when it's done. Think of this as documenting that foreignness we just talked about. Learning how to capture that experience—specifically the process of identifying the emotions associated with it—is a critical part of rebuilding your brain's prediction machine. This is especially true for managing discomfort, anxiety, and fear. Get in the habit of writing down your before and after experiences.

2. Observing Reactions in Others: When you change your behavior, it is reasonable to assume that those people in your work or life around you will notice. As they notice, they might react or respond. Sometimes they do so overtly by letting you

know. At other times, their responses might be more subtle. Learning to pay attention to these reactions will give you an idea of how your shifts might be perceived by others. Write these down and keep a note of any changes you see.

3. Learning to Ask: Recall that pro-social behavior is some of the most biologically rewarding behavior we can engage in. Involving others in our change journey reinforces our motivation and gives access to their feedback. But we must learn to ask. Learning to ask directly and specifically for feedback on how you're approaching change is an important part of filling in the spaces that we cannot observe about ourselves. Asking also does something altruistic for others—it gives them permission to explore their own change objectives. When we declare to others that we are working on change and seeking feedback, we increase their curiosity to do the same.

A CASE STUDY ILLUSTRATION

One thing I've historically not been very good at is selling. You might find this ironic given my nearly lifelong career as a consultant. But it's true. I never liked the relationship side of the job. Dinners with clients. Schmoozing. Going to conferences and introducing myself to new people. Asking them what they do. And so on. It all felt superficial to me. Honestly, it felt borderline manipulative. Like I was using people as a means to an end. I needed to hit my sales numbers, and they were the potential opportunities to do that. At least that was the story I told myself.

I was far more comfortable working on delivery. I loved working with clients, but didn't like selling to them. I was often the guy who would come in towards the end of the sale as "the expert" who was going to do the work. Being credible was important to me. As a result, I often looked a bit sideways at the people who were the account leaders, judgingly viewing them as if they didn't really do any work. They were, I thought, just there to find people who did.

As you can see, this was a narrow, and negative, view. Recall from

Chapter 8 how I shared a story about how my response to the three questions led me to starting my own company. What I didn't share was what happened next. You see, as we've learned, the three questions only take us through the first two phases. At the end of my three questions, here was my From-To statement:

"*From* resting in the safety of big companies *To* embracing the fear and exhilaration of pursuing my passion to help people change their lives."

Creating my own company was simply the medium for bringing this shift to life. It was no longer a question of what I needed to do. The only matter left was to determine how I was going to do it. I knew I couldn't pursue this purpose by working for someone else. So much so, in fact, that I actually stopped an interview with another company in the middle of the interview. I just knew in my heart that I had to do my own thing. But there was one small problem with this realization. I didn't like to sell. It turns out that when you run your own company if you don't sell work, you don't get paid. At all. So, I got to work.

The first step was to identify the verbs I needed to track. I knew the outcome was that I needed to sell consulting projects. The problem was, due to my general dislike of "selling", I had not really developed the skills necessary to sell. Someone usually did it for me. So, the first thing I did was reframe my mindset around selling (Phase 2, Step 4—Motivation and Mindset). Instead of needing to sell, I needed to find clients, people who had the problem I solve. I am good at helping people, teams, and companies change. Really good at it. So, I didn't need to sell people on the idea of it. I needed to find people who needed to change. By the way, one thing I learned along my journey is that I didn't like to sell because I was selling services I didn't believe in just so I could make my annual targets. It turns out that, for me and many others, when I believe deeply in my purpose and I'm sharing my skills to truly help others (not just make money) it feels much better than selling just to make money.

Then I was clear about what I was going to give up. Safety. It's in the From. I could no longer rest on the certainty of a corporate salary. I had to give up safety. I'd like to point out that part of what made this even more terrifying was that, one, I am divorced and have financial obligations that need to be met. And two, I am remarried, and my wife was three months pregnant at the time. If there was ever a moment to run for safety, this was it. But I knew I couldn't go back. This, by the way, was the kind of intense stress that released adrenaline and acetylcholine in my body and brain. Remember, those two hormones are critical to the experience of focus and learning. It was, in fact, the magnitude of the stress of the moment that created my ability to focus. Literally, nothing else mattered. Talk about a narrow field of view!

I had three verbs that I knew I needed to track: share, connect, and embrace. First, I needed to share more of myself, my point of view, with the world. To make the dating analogy, I needed to "put myself out there." This meant sharing ideas on LinkedIn, posting on social media, doing more video, and so on. Second, I needed to connect with as many new people as I could. I would only find people who had the problem I solve if I met more and more people. And third, I needed to embrace the extreme discomfort and uncertainty of this situation.

I gave myself a two-month window to start. Using the Day-Week-Month model, I set the following effort targets:

- Day: I was going to reach out to twenty-five new people per day on LinkedIn.

- Week: Each week, I would post at least two pieces of content on social media.

- Month: Each month I would host two one-hour mastermind sessions with new connections to introduce them to me and my services.

I want to be clear that I had never, ever, done anything like this before. This was about as opposite of my established pattern as I could get. But I knew I had to put effort into building new connections and relationships if my business was going to survive. Heck, if I and my family were going to survive. I'm happy to report that I met every one of those effort goals in the first two months. Let me share with you what happened.

To help with the goal of connecting with more people, I used some automation software that performs outreach on social media. This is quite common these days, but it was new to me. I was going to use automation to reach out to strangers on LinkedIn and introduce myself. Without me being involved in the initial outreach? Oddly, some people would find this easier than an in-person introduction but, for me, I found the idea that automation was making connections was uncomfortable. But people quickly started connecting. Then, some would decline the invitation to connect. I'd get hit with a quick spark of anxiety. I'd tell myself to just keep going. I quickly started to grow my network. But then I had to follow up with these people. I must have had the same (mostly the same) conversation 100 times. But each conversation was a repetition where I learned what felt natural, what felt strange, what people responded to, what they didn't. I varied my responses and replies. All with the goal of making errors and learning from them. And I made some errors for sure.

I found posting content twice per week to be a little easier. It's something I had done some of in the past. I will say that the anxiety here was a little different. One of the things that happens when you post content, at least initially, is that, well, not much happens. Maybe you get a few "likes" or replies. But mostly, you put a lot of effort into an article or post and send it off to the world and . . . silence. Even so, you must keep going. I was doing it for the purpose of getting a specific response. I was doing it to test various approaches. In addition to posting on places like LinkedIn, I did a series of podcasts (also by connecting with strangers who have podcasts) and posted videos.

The monthly mastermind class was far and away the most difficult. I'd generally invite eight to ten people to each session. These are folks I met through my new twenty-five-per-day connection goal. Often, I'd get two-to-three attendees. Once I got only one. But I had to keep going. Much like my son's hitting coach, I had to execute a "good at bat." I had done everything I could to execute with quality. My focus was to now learn from that event to understand what I needed to adjust.

During this two-month period, I added some stress management strategies to complement my behavior changes. First, I took a cold shower every day. This two-minute experience helped me build a resilience that served me well in dealing with the stress of these new actions. Learning to breathe through stress is applicable in many situations. Second, I worked hard to maximize my sleep. With so much stress and activity to get my business up and running, I worked hard to emphasize recovery each day.

I made some important observations about the change I was undertaking. First, the way I shifted my mindset from selling to "finding those in need" made a big difference in how I perceived, and experienced, selling itself. It felt more like service than manipulation. I felt less defeated when someone who I had connected with was not interested. It just meant that they didn't have a change problem. Or at least didn't think they did. Second, many of my fears about building new relationships were simply stories I had told myself. In fact, I was pretty good at it. Anxiety, fear, and disappointment all happen in the relationship-building process. But so do connection, curiosity, and success. Third, when I embraced a growth mindset, if I made a mistake, I simply learned from it. I started to learn that there are people out there who need help and have tried everything, yet nothing has worked. Many of those conversations and connections were the motivation for this book. I knew I couldn't connect with everyone personally. But if I could write it down, I could help others. Fourth, when I asked for feedback, people were willing to offer it and help. By involving them in my change journey, I not only got invaluable information, but I created allies who committed to helping me over the long term.

Speaking of the long-term, it's time to move to the last phase. Let's talk about how we build from this point to create long-term, sustained behavior change.

CHAPTER 12

Adapt

"You do not rise to the level of your goals.
You fall to the level of your systems."
JAMES CLEAR

J AMES CLEAR IS THE PROUD RECIPIENT of two quotes in this book. This one is my favorite. It speaks to what I have hoped to accomplish. To give you a formula for how to build a change system that you can apply across multiple dimensions of your life, from work to health to relationships. I've helped thousands of people change across many types of organizations, and one thing I've become more and more certain of is this. We cannot lead others, whether it's our family, friends, or coworkers, through change until we have designed a system for ourselves. That is the central goal of this book—to build your ability to change by giving you a formula to build a system for change. One that leverages the unique attributes of your human brain and experience to increase your chances of success.

The Adapt Phase is where we put it all together. It's where we take what we've learned from Adopt and lean on our new knowledge, insight, experience, and errors to build our change system. Like learning a foreign language, this is our study abroad. We move from the classroom to an immersive experience of change. We move out of the change lab and into the world to apply what we've learned in a systematic way.

In the Adopt Phase, we were applying the six science-backed strategies. In this phase, our goal is to make change a habit. That's right. A habit. Our goal is to embed your ability to change as a skill in and of itself. We are building adaptation in us just as we would a muscle. Shift by shift, action by action, error by error, reflection by reflection, we create a repeatable pattern in our brains and bodies that can handle an ever-increasing number of adaptations. Whether it's a goal to improve your health or your relationships, or to lead your company through transformation, you will unlock unlimited potential in yourself. And ultimately in those you lead.

THE ADAPT PROCESS

All the science we have learned comes together here. We put it all together. Rather than restate those principles, we'll jump right into the four primary steps required to adapt: 1) adjusting from learnings and errors, 2) creating support structures, 3) designing your change intervals, and 4) building the habit of change. Let's jump right in.

STEP 1
Adjusting from Adopt Phase Learnings.

At the end of the Adopt Phase we documented what we learned from the effort we applied towards our change goals. Remember, our intent is to make effort the reward. To strive towards goals without worrying about the outcome, and to instead focus on the effort required to achieve the goal. Recall that the Reward Paradox is that we want the outcomes of goals, but not always the effort required to achieve them. We start this phase by leveraging a technique we already know—our three questions. However, instead of using these three questions to evaluate our goals, we use them to evaluate the experience of giving the effort required to achieve them.

The first question is to review your approach to goal pursuit in the Adopt phase. How did you show effort in pursuit of your goals? A simple review of your day-week-month approach is sufficient here. The second question is, "How did that effort serve you in pursuit of your goals?" Here, we evaluate the results of delivering that effort. We evaluate whether it was easy or hard and whether we stuck to our day-week-month format or struggled to meet even a minimum of effort. More importantly, we evaluate how we dealt with the stress and discomfort of making the effort. Did we need a lot of support? Were we able to "dig deep" when needed? Did we find the effort getting harder or easier? And finally, the third question: "How might you do it differently?" Here is where we determine any adjustments needed based on those observations. Think of it as a three-question sprint. Again, the more feedback you can get from others, the better.

There's a general rule for the adjustments you choose. They should not be easier. Let me clarify this. Recall that we need to do hard things for our anterior mid-cingulate cortex to grow. Hard, of course, is relative. Let's say your Day goal was five minutes of meditation as part of a self-care routine. If you were able to easily meet that commitment each day, you might consider doubling or tripling it. The idea is to increase, not decrease, the effort. At the same time, there is a difference between something being difficult and counterproductive. Just like exercise should be hard but not painful, so too should your behavior-change efforts. If you're making a change that comes at the expense of your relationships, well, that's counterproductive. One way of determining this is to again ask the people closest to you if they are feeling any negative effects from the efforts you're making.

STEP 2
Creating support structures

Your next task is to create the support structures needed for your long-term adaptation effort. In step 1 you should learn why, when, and where your effort fell short. Perhaps you're not as good at the morning workout as you thought. Perhaps you struggle to modulate your stress response when in a disagreement. Perhaps you struggle to ask for help when anxiety kicks in. Whatever the reason, now is the time to create structures around you to support you, both in times of struggle and to accelerate your effort.

To start, look no further than the first science-backed strategy,

Shift Environment. Your physical environment is often the most straightforward environment to address. First, start by creating constraints which make it more difficult to perform behaviors you wish to suppress. A simple example might be turning the Wi-Fi off or putting your phone in another room in your home at a certain time to ensure you don't scroll and get to bed. Next, identify ways to shift your physical environment to make your desired behavior easier. An example is setting your workout clothes the night before to make it easier to exercise first thing in the morning. Or replacing processed junk foods with fruit to avoid snacking on unhealthy options.

One of the most important environmental shifts to make here is your social environment. The most direct example are social groups organized around activities or hobbies that match your adaptation goals. Social interaction increases motivation and helps us keep broader commitments to our change efforts. While in person is ideal, these groups can be effective virtually, depending on your goals.

Certainly, if those support groups are available, leverage them to the greatest extent possible. If not, involve a friend, loved one, counselor, or coach in your process. This is especially important for what I call "moments of weakness." Each of us is familiar with the "I don't want to" conversation in our head anytime we must do something we simply don't want to. This conversation can last seconds, minutes, or hours. When we involve another person in that conversation, we must listen to ourselves say out loud that we are not willing to give the effort needed to change. Some call this an accountability partner. I'm not a huge fan of that term. It tends to lean towards the negative in its connotation. Instead, I call this a vulnerability partner. When we give language to our struggle, and we get feedback from others in the process, we open the possibility for neuroplasticity by acknowledging that we are unable, unwilling, or both, to address the errors in our behaviors.

The final important support structure is, quite simply, your health and well-being. If I had to give you one recommendation for supporting your long-term change aspirations, it is to improve your sleep. Sleep is the foundation of recovery and learning. Pulling all-nighters and pushing hard all the time will not help you physically, behaviorally, relationally, or emotionally. Of course, exercise and diet are a close second and third. But if you had to pick one, and only one, I'd start with sleep.

STEP 3
Designing your change intervals

With your adjustments identified and your structures in place, you're likely asking, "Well, how long do I go before I make another adjustment?" It's a great question. In Phase Three, our timeline was no more than two months. That's enough time for the initial test of our change efforts to determine how we need to adjust . . . but not enough to fully change.

My starting point for a timeline is three months. There is data to support that creating a goal-pursuit window aligned to seasonal schedules can have positive effects on our motivation. It's also easy to remember the big seasonal changes. The other reason I like this approach is that the seasons don't align perfectly with the calendar. That small offset can be helpful in avoiding the Quitter's Day trap. But any three-month interval will do.

In addition, try to keep one goal for each three-month interval. Again, the intent is not to accomplish the goal in three months. The intent is to set an effort horizon over a three-month period. Within the three-month period, adjusting the day-week-month structure is perfectly fine. This helps us avoid the messy middle problem of goal pursuit.

The challenge here is to balance consistency with change. Remember, you should be addressing a behavior that, up to this point, has been a habit. Changing this behavior will not happen overnight. Recall the figure from Chapter 1 that displays a continuum with habit on one end and change on the other. In these effort cycles, you are creating focused, consistent effort on a new pattern of behavior that moves you away from a habit and into a new manner of behaving. We need consistency of this new behavior to create the long-term potentiation required to repurpose a neural pathway, as well as long-term depression (i.e., not performing) of the old behavior. Remember that NOT engaging in the old behavior is as important as performing the new one. Revisit the steps outlined in

Chapter 3, Initiate Movement, for ways to structure this interval.

What most people wonder by this point is, "how will I know I have moved from habit to change?" The answer lies in what we learned about stress in Chapter 4. Here's the basic principle to follow: the easier something is for you to do, the more it is a habit. The harder something is to do, the less so. Here's a simple example. For the better part of your entire life, you've been brushing your teeth with your dominant hand. And you've been doing so in a particular pattern. You've done it so much that you don't have to think about it. In fact, it is so automatic that you can think about, and do, something else like your to-do list while you do it. If you were to switch to brushing your teeth with your non-dominant hand, and in a different pattern, you would likely feel a deep sense of frustration. First, you'd have to really think about it. Your mind would not be on your to-do list at all. You'd be intently focused on the movement and pattern which, unsurprisingly, will be far less fluid and effective. That frustration would create the sensation that the two-minute experience lasted ten minutes or more. Recall that frustration and stress result in a finer slicing of time and the perception that time extends. However, if you kept brushing your teeth with your non-dominant hand, you'd get a little better each time until, eventually, you'd be able to think about it less. How long would that take? It's hard to tell, but it would certainly take longer than you wanted. At some point, you'd be tempted to go back to your dominant hand. You should only move on to your next change goal when you've reached a sufficiently low level of stress in the new behavior that there is no danger of reverting to the old behavior.

STEP 4
Building the habit of change.

I mentioned earlier in this book that I've been known to Jedi mind trick my clients. I must admit, I've been doing it again. To this point, I've given you a great deal of information on how to change, from the questions to help you identify what to change, to the process for how to bring about change. You've hopefully followed along and defined your own change goals that you'll address when you're done with this book. It's common to find the big things in life that are holding you back and put those at the top of the change list. After all, why go through all this trouble if your change goal is small potatoes? But it's time for me to come clean. I don't care what you change. I just care that you change. Something. Anything. Whether it's a deeply held belief that is holding you back in life or brushing your teeth with your other hand. It is the *practice of changing* that is most important. And here's the second admission. What this book is really about is what I call "The Habit of Change." It is a formula for change that can, and should, be applied to your life over and over and over again.

It is our unwillingness to change that most often stops us from changing. It is the all-or-nothing mindset that keeps us where we are. When we make change a habit, we self-induce disruption in our lives that unlocks our potential. We move from the passenger's seat to the driver's seat. We constantly and continuously find new ways to challenge ourselves to greater heights. And the moment we look around and feel the comfort of our current situation, we know it's time to change. When change is a habit, we continuously raise the bar and create multiple inflection points in our life. Adaptability becomes the behavior we seek. The moment we feel stagnation taking hold is the moment we scan and find an opportunity to change.

So, how do you know when change has become a habit? First, the stress associated with change is not enough to deter you from change. You're able to embrace the stress and discomfort of change without giving up. Second, you are the one who initiates change in your life. It doesn't come from an external source. Third, no area of life is out of out of bounds for your change efforts. You are more able to evaluate the entire spectrum of your behavior and being deeply honest with yourself. And fourth, the moment that one change becomes a habit, you find another. The pursuit of change never ends.

THE CASE STUDY OF YOU

We've covered a lot of ground, from a foundation of science and neuroscience about the brain and body, to six key principles that promote change, to a four-step process to put it into practice. Now that we know, we must act on what we know.

To change, we must build a system that supports our ability to change. Time and time again. If we are to build the habit of change, that must help us:

- Reflect on the three questions to identify the behaviors in your life that are holding you back.

- Identify your new change goals by designing From-To statements which give you something to pursue, not just avoid.

- Shift the physical, virtual, emotional, and social environments around you to create constraints and access towards your goals.

- Initiate movement and leverage strategies to maintain your motivation.

- Intentionally do hard things to harness the power of your anterior mid-cingulate cortex (aMCC) to embrace and realize the positive effects of short-term stress.

- Create focus to maximize the alertness, energy, and attention required to learn new behaviors.

- Decide what you want to unlearn, as much as what we want to learn.

- Adopt and test new behaviors through both repetition and failure to open neuroplasticity.

- Redefine effort as the reward of change.

- Design change intervals and use the three questions to continuously self-induce change.

- Develop and employ a growth mindset.

It is this last component, growth mindset, that warrants additional attention before you start your journey. As was demonstrated through research, when we adopt a "stress-is-enhancing" and "growth" mindset, we do two things. First, we lessen the intensity of the stress we experience during change. Second, we increase our chances of transformation success.

I want to give you four specific variations of these mindsets which will guide you on your transformation journey:

Acknowledge: The sooner we resolve that change is coming, and that change will be difficult, the more we prime our brain and body for the experience. It's not just acknowledging that stress is good for you, it's acknowledging that stress is required for growth. If we think back to our Adaptation graphic from the Introduction, this acknowledgement moves the inflection point of our change experience to the left.

Anticipate: When we anticipate difficult moments, we interrupt our brain's prediction machine and are better prepared for uncertain events. This is not about expecting the worst. It's about strategizing and preparing for obstacles so we do not give up when our change experience doesn't match our brain's prediction.

Persevere: Without question, change requires endurance and resilience. Your commitment to persevere through change is essential. Change requires that when we get knocked down, we get back up. Change always takes longer than we hope. We must keep pressing on.

Challenge: Change requires that we challenge ourselves, particularly as it relates to many of our deeply held beliefs. This doesn't mean you need to change those beliefs per se. It means we must be open to the idea that our current beliefs and behaviors may no longer serve us. Challenge yourself to examine every aspect of your life.

I will leave you here with your future in your hands. Unwritten. Waiting to be changed and adapted using the strategies and techniques discussed in this book. Here's to change. To your journey. To uncomfortable, terrifying, scary, exhilarating, limitless transformation.

And here's to the you that sits on the other side.

FREE GIFT FOR READERS

 s a reader of *Change*, I've provided a free downloadable *Change Workbook* to support you on your change journey. You can access it here:
https://www.michaeljlopez.coach/change

FROM–TO STATEMENTS

Health & Wellness

From: Being twenty pounds overweight.
To: Increasing my energy and vitality through regular exercise.

From: Being too busy to prioritize healthy foods.
To: Making healthy choices that increase my lifespan.

From: Prioritizing others over myself.
To: Acknowledging self-care is an investment in my ability to care for others.

From: Living in a state of constant stress.
To: Developing strategies to manage and leverage positive stress towards my goals.

Relationships

From: Being too distracted.
To: Setting aside dedicated, focused time for my most important relationship.

From: Focusing on my frustrations with my partner.
To: Learning how I can be the best version of myself for them.

From: Reserving only small amounts of time for my kids.
To: Treating parenting as a priority on par with professional obligations.

From: Reacting emotionally to negative situations (e.g., argument).
To: Pausing to listen and understand before responding.

Career

From: Working more than I desire.
To: Balancing work and life to ensure I maintain a healthy lifestyle.

From: Exclusively defining myself through my career goals.
To: Valuing the totality of my contributions and impact in work, family, friendships and beyond.

From: Consistently focusing on my next promotion opportunity.
To: Acknowledging self-care is an investment in my ability to care for others.

From: Being a manager who is doing the work.
To: Delegating and empowering my team to do the work.

Financial

From: Spending beyond my means.
To: Prioritizing and budgeting against my most important goals.

From: Making financial gain my primary focus.
To: Understanding that money is an enabler to a full life.

From: Defining my value through my salary.
To: Appreciating my emotional, social, and relational contributions to the most important people in my life.

From: Seeing money as a source of persistent stress.
To: Developing a healthy relationship with money as one of several tools to support my goals.

END NOTES

Introduction

"Successful Transformations." McKinsey & Company, 8 Oct. 2021.

Achim Buschmeyer, Günther Schuh, Daniel Wentzel, Organizational Transformation Towards Product-service Systems—Empirical Evidence in Managing the Behavioral Transformation Process, Procedia CIRP, Volume 47, 2016.

Higgins-Dunn, Noah, and Christina Farr. "How Zoom Rose to the Top During the Coronavirus Pandemic." CNBC, 3 Apr. 2020, https://www.cnbc.com/2020/04/03/how-zoom-rose-to-the-top-during-the-coronavirus-pandemic.html

Tudor, Christina (2022), "The Impact of the COVID-19 Pandemic on the Global Web and Video Conferencing SaaS Market", International Business and Economics Department, Bucharest University of Economic Studies: 2022

Chapter 1

Barrett, Lisa Feldman. Seven and a Half Lessons About the Brain. Houghton Mifflin Harcourt, 2020

Barrett, Lisa Feldman. How Emotions Are Made: The Secret Life of the Brain. Houghton Mifflin Harcourt, 2017

Wood, Wendy. Good Habits, Bad Habits: The Science of Making Positive Changes That Stick. Farrar, Straus and Giroux, 2019

"Habit." Merriam-Webster.com Dictionary, Merriam-Webster, https://www.merriam-webster.com/dictionary/habit. Accessed May 2024

Huberman, Andrew, host. "How to Increase Your Willpower and Tenacity." Huberman Lab, 28 Aug. 2023, https://www.hubermanlab.com/episode/how-to-increase-your-willpower-and-tenacity

Job, Veronika, et al. "Beliefs About Willpower Determine the Impact of Glucose on Self-Control." Proceedings of the National Academy of Sciences, vol. 110, no. 37, 2013, pp. 14837-14842, https://doi.org/10.1073/pnas.1313475110

Crum, A. J., Salovey, P., & Achor, S. (2013). Rethinking stress: The role of mindsets in determining the stress response. Journal of Personality and Social Psychology, 104(4), 716–733. https://doi.org/10.1037/a0031201

Touroutoglou, Alexandra, et al. "The Tenacious Brain: How the Anterior Mid-Cingulate Contributes to Achieving Goals." Cortex, vol. 123, 2019, pp. 12-29, https://doi.org/10.1016/j.cortex.2019.09.011

Chapter 2

"Choice Overload Bias." The Decision Lab, https://thedecisionlab.com/biases/choice-overload-bias. Accessed March 2024

Chernev, Alexander, Ulf Böckenholt, and Joseph Goodman. "Choice Overload: A Conceptual Review and Meta-Analysis." Journal of Consumer Psychology, vol. 25, no. 2, 2015, pp. 333-358, https://doi.org/10.1016/j.jcps.2014.08.002

Zhenjing G, Chupradit S, Ku KY, Nassani AA, Haffar M. Impact of Employees' Workplace Environment on Employees' Performance: A Multi-Mediation Model. Front Public Health. 2022 May 13;10:890400. doi: 10.3389/fpubh.2022.890400. PMID: 35646787; PMCID: PMC9136218.

Duhigg, Charles. "What Google Learned from Its Quest to Build the Perfect Team." The New York Times Magazine, 25 Feb. 2016, https://www.nytimes.com/2016/02/28/magazine/what-google-learned-from-its-quest-to-build-the-perfect-team.html

"Dr. Robert Malenka: How Your Brain's Reward Circuits Drive Your Choices." Huberman Lab, hosted by Andrew Huberman, 2023, https://www.hubermanlab.com/episode/dr-robert-malenka-how-your-brains-reward-circuits-drive-your-choices?timestamp=4769

Dai B, Sun F, Tong X, Ding Y, Kuang A, Osakada T, Li Y, Lin D. Responses and functions of dopamine in nucleus accumbens core during social behaviors. Cell Rep. 2022 Aug 23;40(8):111246. doi: 10.1016/j.celrep.2022.111246. PMID: 36001967; PMCID: PMC9511885.

Trezza V, Campolongo P, Vanderschuren LJ. Evaluating the rewarding nature of social interactions in laboratory animals. Dev Cogn Neurosci. 2011 Oct;1(4):444-58. doi: 10.1016/j.dcn.2011.05.007. Epub 2011 Jun 2. PMID: 22436566; PMCID: PMC6987553

Larrabee Sonderlund A, Thilsing T, Sondergaard J. Should social disconnectedness be included in primary-care screening for cardiometabolic disease? A systematic review of the relationship between everyday stress, social connectedness, and allostatic load. PLoS One. 2019 Dec 19;14(12):e0226717. doi: 10.1371/journal.pone.0226717. PMID: 31856249; PMCID: PMC6922387.

Smith ML, Asada N, Malenka RC. Anterior cingulate inputs to nucleus accumbens control the social transfer of pain and analgesia. Science. 2021 Jan 8;371(6525):153-159. doi: 10.1126/science.abe3040. Epub 2021 Jan 7. PMID: 33414216; PMCID: PMC7952019

Chapter 3

Hershfield, Hal, Stephen Shu, and Shlomo Benartzi. "Temporal Reframing and Participation in a Savings Program: A Field Experiment." 2 Feb. 2019, https://doi.org/10.2139/ssrn.3097464

Shankar, Maya. "Avoidance vs. Approach-Oriented Goals." Tactics Plus, https://tacticsplus.com/tools/productivity/avoidance-vs-approach-oriented-goals-tools-by-maya-shankar/. Accessed April 2024.

"All About Motivation." Usable Knowledge, Harvard Graduate School of Education, 14 Sept. 2018, https://www.gse.harvard.edu/ideas/usable-knowledge/18/09/all-about-motivation

Hull, Clark L. "The Goal-Gradient Hypothesis and Maze Learning." Psychological Review, vol. 39, no. 1, 1932, pp. 25-43, https://doi.org/10.1037/h0072640

Cook, D. B., et al. "Functional Neuroimaging Correlates of Mental Fatigue Induced by Cognition Among Chronic Fatigue Syndrome Patients and Controls." NeuroImage, vol. 36, no. 1, 2007, pp. 108-122, https://doi.org/10.1016/j.neuroimage.2007.02.033

Hakim H, Khemiri A, Chortane OG, Boukari S, Chortane SG, Bianco A, Marsigliante S, Patti A, Muscella A. Mental Fatigue Effects on the Produced Perception of Effort and Its Impact on Subsequent Physical Performances. Int J Environ Res Public Health. 2022 Sep 2;19(17):10973. doi: 10.3390/ijerph191710973. PMID: 36078686; PMCID: PMC9517922.

Kappes, Heather Barry, and Gabriele Oettingen. "Positive Fantasies About Idealized Futures Sap Energy." Journal of Experimental Social Psychology, vol. 47, no. 4, 2011, pp. 719-729, https://doi.org/10.1016/j.jesp.2011.02.003

Huberman, Andrew. "Tools to Manage Dopamine and Improve Motivation and Drive." Huberman Lab, https://www.hubermanlab.com/newsletter/tools-to-manage-dopamine-and-improve-motivation-and-drive. Accessed June 2023.

Chapter 4

Selye, H. (1956). The stress of life. McGraw-Hill

"General Adaptation Syndrome: What It Is, Stages, and Examples." Healthline, https://www.healthline.com/health/general-adaptation-syndrome#definition. Accessed June 2024.

"Understanding the Stress Response." Harvard Health Publishing, 2018, https://www.health.harvard.edu/staying-healthy/understanding-the-stress-response. Accessed May 2024.

"General Adaptation Syndrome: What It Is, Stages, and Examples." Healthline, https://www.healthline.com/health/general-adaptation-syndrome#stages. Accessed June 2024.

Baldi E, Bucherelli C. The Inverted "U-Shaped" Dose-Effect Relationships in Learning and Memory: Modulation of Arousal and Consolidation. Nonlinearity in Biology, Toxicology, Medicine. 2005;3(1). doi:10.2201/nonlin.003.01.002

Yeager, D.S., Bryan, C.J., Gross, J.J. et al. A synergistic mindsets intervention protects adolescents from stress. Nature 607, 512–520 (2022). https://doi.org/10.1038/s41586-022-04907-7

Chapter 5

Wurtz RH. Recounting the impact of Hubel and Wiesel. J Physiol. 2009 Jun 15;587(Pt 12):2817-23. doi: 10.1113/jphysiol.2009.170209. PMID: 19525566; PMCID: PMC2718241.

TEDx Talks. "The Science of Productivity | Dr. Sahar Yousef | TEDxBerkeley." YouTube, 20 Jan. 2015, https://www.youtube.com/watch?v=It8SJQkseHE

"How to Focus to Change Your Brain." Huberman Lab, hosted by Andrew Huberman, 12 Apr. 2021, https://www.hubermanlab.com/episode/how-to-focus-to-change-your-brain

Kilgard MP, Merzenich MM. Cortical map reorganization enabled by nucleus basalis activity. Science. 1998 Mar 13;279(5357):1714-8. doi: 10.1126/science.279.5357.1714. PMID: 9497289

Chapter 6

Purves D, Augustine GJ, Fitzpatrick D, et al., editors. Neuroscience. 2nd edition. Sunderland (MA): Sinauer Associates; 2001. Long-Term Synaptic Potentiation. Available from: https://www.ncbi.nlm.nih.gov/books/NBK10878/

Collingridge, G., Peineau, S., Howland, J. et al. Long-term depression in the CNS. Nat Rev Neurosci 11, 459–473 (2010). https://doi.org/10.1038/nrn2867

Barkan CL, Zornik E. Feedback to the future: motor neuron contributions to central pattern generator function. J Exp Biol. 2019 Aug 16;222(Pt 16):jeb193318. doi: 10.1242/jeb.193318. PMID: 31420449; PMCID: PMC6739810

Zayia LC, Tadi P. Neuroanatomy, Motor Neuron. [Updated 2023 Jul 24]. In: StatPearls [Internet]. Treasure Island (FL): StatPearls Publishing; 2024 Jan-. Available from: https://www.ncbi.nlm.nih.gov/books/NBK554616/

Barkan CL, Zornik E. Feedback to the future: motor neuron contributions to central pattern generator function. J Exp Biol. 2019 Aug 16;222(Pt 16):jeb193318. doi: 10.1242/jeb.193318. PMID: 31420449; PMCID: PMC6739810.

Norman KJ, Riceberg JS, Koike H, Bateh J, McCraney SE, Caro K, Kato D, Liang A, Yamamuro K, Flanigan ME, Kam K, Falk EN, Brady DM, Cho C, Sadahiro M, Yoshitake K, Maccario P, Demars MP, Waltrip L, Varga AW, Russo SJ, Baxter MG, Shapiro ML, Rudebeck PH, Morishita H. Post-error recruitment of frontal sensory cortical projections promotes attention in mice. Neuron. 2021 Apr 7;109(7):1202-1213. e5. doi: 10.1016/j.neuron.2021.02.001. Epub 2021 Feb 19. PMID: 33609483; PMCID: PMC8035262.

Feldman DE, Knudsen EI. An anatomical basis for visual calibration of the auditory space map in the barn owl's midbrain. J Neurosci. 1997 Sep 1;17(17):6820-37. doi: 10.1523/JNEUROSCI.17-17-06820.1997. PMID: 9254692; PMCID: PMC6573134.

Brainard MS, Knudsen EI. Sensitive periods for visual calibration of the auditory space map in the barn owl optic tectum. J Neurosci. 1998 May 15;18(10):3929-42. doi: 10.1523/JNEUROSCI.18-10-03929.1998. PMID: 9570820; PMCID: PMC6793138.

Thibodeaux, Wanda. "Why Working in 90-Minute Intervals Is Powerful for Your Body and Job." Inc., 7 Nov. 2017, https://www.inc.com/wanda-thibodeaux/why-working-in-90-minute-intervals-is-powerful-for-your-body-and-job-according-t.html

"How to Learn Skills Faster." Huberman Lab, hosted by Andrew Huberman, 26 July 2021, https://www.hubermanlab.com/episode/how-to-learn-skills-faster

Chapter 7

"Time Perception and Entrainment by Dopamine, Serotonin, and Hormones." Huberman Lab, hosted by Andrew Huberman, 14 Feb. 2022, https://www.hubermanlab.com/episode/time-perception-and-entrainment-by-dopamine-serotonin-and-hormones

"Dr. Robert Malenka: How Your Brain's Reward Circuits Drive Your Choices." Huberman Lab, hosted by Andrew Huberman, 22 May 2023, https://www.hubermanlab.com/episode/dr-robert-malenka-how-your-brains-reward-circuits-drive-your-choices

Mueller CM, Dweck CS. Praise for intelligence can undermine children's motivation and performance. J Pers Soc Psychol. 1998 Jul;75(1):33-52. doi: 10.1037//0022-3514.75.1.33. PMID: 9686450.

Lee, Christopher R., Alon Chen, and Kay M. Tye. "The Neural Circuitry of Social Homeostasis: Consequences of Acute Versus Chronic Social Isolation." Cell, vol. 184, no. 6, 2021, pp. 1500-1516, https://doi.org/10.1016/j.cell.2021.02.028

Lee CR, Chen A, Tye KM. The neural circuitry of social homeostasis: Consequences of acute versus chronic social isolation. Cell. 2021 Mar 18;184(6):1500-1516. doi: 10.1016/j.cell.2021.02.028. Epub 2021 Mar 9. Erratum in: Cell. 2021 May 13;184(10):2794-2795. doi: 10.1016/j.cell.2021.04.044. PMID: 33691140; PMCID: PMC8580010

About the Author

MICHAEL J. LÓPEZ is a transformative coach dedicated to empowering companies, leaders, teams, and individuals to enhance performance through meaningful change. As a top voice and thought leader in the realm of change management, Michael adopts a bold and candid approach, helping clients identify and dismantle the barriers that prevent them from realizing their full potential.

At the core of Michael's purpose as a coach are three key obligations. First, he is committed to honesty, challenging individuals and organizations with ideas, concepts, and conversations that may be uncomfortable but are essential for growth. Second, he provides guidance through these challenging experiences, offering strategies and tactics to foster development. Finally, Michael leads by example, applying the same concepts, strategies, and tactics he shares in his own life—at work, in relationships, in friendships, and as a parent.

Utilizing scientific principles, Michael elucidates the necessity of change and explores the personal characteristics that inhibit growth. He teaches how to embrace basic principles of human behavior to welcome change into one's life, fostering an environment where growth can thrive. His ultimate goal is to help both organizations and individuals advance farther and faster.

Michael has a proven track record of delivering results across various industries and business models. A dedicated student of "the human industry," he blends his passion for the science and practice of behavior change to craft innovative strategies that drive transformation. His leadership style is diverse, shaped by his experiences in business, civil service, military, and athletics, which he leverages to accelerate performance for leaders and teams alike.

In 2023, Michael started a boutique consultancy focused exclusively on helping organizations transform. Prior to this, he held senior leadership positions at Prophet Consulting, KPMG, and Ernst & Young following a significant tenure of thirteen years with Booz Allen Hamilton. Most recently, Michael served at Prophet Consulting. He also held the position of Director of Innovation & Strategy at Smiths Interconnect, a global diversified industrial products company, and began his career as an Intelligence Officer in the U.S. Intelligence Community.

Michael holds an MBA from George Mason University and a BA from Occidental College. A former college athlete, he is actively involved in sports, serving on the Leadership Council of the Positive Coaching Alliance and coaching youth and high school football. This is truly who he is—a committed coach and change agent.

www.ingramcontent.com/pod-product-compliance
Lightning Source LLC
Chambersburg PA
CBHW071718140626
46557CB00012B/952